MW01226677

DEFENSE IS BETTER THAN OFFENSE

HELLO! MY NAME IS OVERCOMER

GOOD GRIEF!

THE TRUTH THAT SET ME FREE

STILL STANDING

LOST AND FOUND

ProdiGALS

DAUGHTERS OF DESTINY

Table of Contents

Daughter of Destiny

There's an old song that says "the devil thought he had me, but I got away"

I'm standing here a living testimony, proving His great power to you today

To show you all that, though my path wasn't the straight and narrow, the Lord made a way

He didn't let me lay in the ditch nor the pit, instead He brought me home to stay

He swaddled me in grace and mercy and called me by name

He showed me that I was set apart, me and this world are not the same

His footprints are found in the deep grooves of the road I traveled, in which I never should have

But it was in those moments that He walked for me; he carried me when I was unable to handle the aftermath

When I was left to deal with the consequence of my own choices, He still showed up to lend me His hand

He still would will for the enemy to release his grip from me and give me another chance

His DNA never left my heart, his fingerprints are evident in my life

Even when I was at my lowest, heavy-ladened and downtrodden, burdened by iniquity and strife

He refused to let me go, because He had great plans for me

From day one, He had already orchestrated my destiny

So, though I chose to mock Him and rebel against what I knew to be true

He showed me agape love and He reminded me of His words that said "I will never forsake you"

Though I had discounted His blood and decided that it was unworthy to cover me

He still made it His will, that there would be a plan for Him to recover me

For I have always been His, I never belonged to this world

From the beginning of my life, at conception, I was his beautiful baby girl

He had planned to use my life, to bring light to others who could not see through their darkness

But I decided that my way was best, my goodness, my head was the hardest

And I was walking around reckless, trying to will my head and my heart to match

But He stood in the gap for me and refused to allow that root of bitterness to latch

Because He knew that once it attached itself to my heart, it would make it that much harder for me to come out

So, He stood between me and myself and warred against unbelief and doubt

He called unto my remembrance the lineage I was from

There was no need to try to prove myself to this world, I had already been ransomed by the One

The One true living God, the Alpha and Omega, my provider and Prince of Peace

I had no choice but to return to sender, because He held the receipt for me

He adorned scars on His back, holes in his wrists and feet

Wounds around His head, that proved the price
He paid for me

So, I had to turn away from this foreign land, this
pig pen that I'd been laying in and find my
Father's house

No matter the cost, I was returning home, I had to
seek Him out

Because otherwise I would have been lost,
without the cross so I refused to continue to
wander around aimlessly

I was going home to my Father's house, returning
a ProdiGAL, a true Daughter of Destiny

PROLOGUE

This book is a collection of testimonies from women who have lived in the world but been born again by the baptism, defined as being completely submerged under water, in the name of Jesus Christ, for the remission of sins. They have also all received the precious gift of the Holy Ghost, evidence by speaking in other tongues.

The idea for this book was birthed one day while Gina was reading a post on social media. She thought about how the testimonies of other people had affected her own life. She planned to write a book herself about this, but then she decided to get some women together instead to tell several testimonies at once. She came up with the name ProdiGALs because unlike the son in the parable in the Bible, they are women. Hence the GAL. The subtitle Daughters of Destiny came to her one day in the process of editing the book and discussing other things with the other women involved with the book. Each woman had their own unique story of how they got on the road to destiny. She thought this was perfect for the stories that they were telling. It was initially her plan to have more women tell their stories, but that didn't happen. However, she is optimistic that ProdiGALs can become a series and maybe even a household name in hopes of rescuing the lost from this dying world.

These brave women, have decided to put pen to paper and share their stories of defeat, destruction and despair, not to glorify the sin but to glorify the God who eradicated those sins from their lives. The testimonies in this book were written in hopes of ministering to a heart that may be broken, a mind that is weary and a body that is tired. It is their prayers that while reading their stories that the reader receives a new revelation of who Jesus is. They want the reader not to see them as the authors, but God as the author and finisher of their faith (Hebrews 12:1-2).

The book begins with Ebony telling of all the things she went through to find God. She explains how she always had this tug, a pull at her heart that there was more out there for her, but she was having trouble finding it. She testifies of her struggles with many abuses from drugs and alcohol to fornication and rebellion but one of the biggest struggles for her was the spirit of offense. In her chapter, she quotes many scriptures so that her readers know that there is word, sound doctrine, to back up anything she is telling them. She gives them the opportunity to read it for themselves. Ebony's chapter shows the world that no matter how low we think we have sunken, Jesus will reach to whatever pit He needs to in order to find you. There isn't a valley low enough that He won't rescue you from.

Next, we have a grueling story of grief written by Kat. She tells of the heaviness she experienced at the loss of her children and husband. She openly describes these experiences and the pain she constantly lived with for years and still struggles with at times. Her transparency is so freeing. It also gives her readers insight into her life. Sometimes I think we take for granted the path God has set us on and we are reminded how blessed we are when we witness the struggles of others. Kat's chapter definitely makes you want to thank God for what you do have and celebrate every victory in your life every time you get the chance because life truly is short.

Then we move on to the chronicle of Catrisha. The way she describes in great detail the things God brought her out of catches the reader by surprise and screams of His grace and mercy. She tells about many experiences in her youth that she struggled with all the way through adulthood. However, she also talks about how the chains of fornication were broken when she decided that Jesus truly was enough and that she could live without fornicating but she couldn't live without Jesus. Her testimony drips with inspiration, saying to its reader, "you can get up from this"! Even when there seems to be no way, there is always a way made in and through Jesus!

Following that powerful testimony, we find the narrative of Courtney. She invites us into the privacy of her struggles with suicide attempts and allows us to see the scars she was left with by wounds that she thought would never heal. She tells us how God stepped in and gave her more than just peace, hope and love but He gave her a new lease on life and new people she would come to call family. Courtney delivers to us, the factors that set her on a path to ending it all. She also counters that with how the power of God set her free from the chains on her mind. To see her today, you would never think that this lively, bubbly spirit could have ever had the thought to take her own life. But God!

After prayer and support from her leadership, Amber submitted her chapter to be a part of this ProdiGAL journey with five other women. Amber delivers to us in intimate detail the grip that addiction had on her life. She also does the same to describe the cleansing power of the blood of Jesus over that very addiction. Over and over in her chapter you find her giving praise to the God of the universe for saving her. You will also find her pouring out her soul to her readers in hopes that they receive what she is saying and change the narrative of how they see an addict in their own lives. She wants every person reading her words to know that no one wants to be an addict. All addicts want to be free from the bondage they are under in addiction, they just don't know how to get out and stay out. She considers herself one of the blessed ones who, by the power of the Holy Ghost, was able to escape the disgusting despair that addiction riddled her life with. She has witnessed too many not have the same fate to remain quiet and not tell the world about what God did for her!

Gina gives an account of how her life was deeply affected by her lack of worthiness, confidence and self-esteem. Surely, many of us can relate to this.

We all have had some unfortunate experience that stemmed from lack. Whether that lack was in confidence, self-esteem, love, finances or some other cause, we have all had some adverse effects because of it. She also speaks to the absence of her father as well as the strain from being in a marriage where she felt they were not prepared for. You can feel the agony that she must have experienced leaping off the pages as she gives her account of some of her life experiences. Her testimony is that of a young girl who never knew any better finding a powerful treasure in the word of God, in the church and in Jesus Himself.

This book is full of adversity, despair, turmoil and trouble. However, all of those things are also countered with grace, mercy, love, redemption and victory. The tales of the women in this book are not just for them, but for the world to see that life can be hard, however Jesus stands mightier than anything that comes against us. No matter what, if we put our lives in His hands, He will always take care of us.

Come and take a journey with these brave, powerful, amazing women and enjoy the testimonies of redemption by 6 daughters of destiny who are truly real-life ProdiGALs!

Offense:

a breach of a law or rule; an illegal act; annoyance or resentment brought about by a perceived insult to or disregard for oneself or one's standards or principles

The spirit of offense is brutal. Sometimes we become offended at things that aren't what they seem; it is simply how we perceived it. The issue with that is that, perception, really is reality. The way I receive something is worth more to me than the way you intended for your words or actions to land with me. It is so important that we are mindful how things land with people because we are just as much at fault for their offense as they are for being offended. I know that sounds unfair, however, to be cliché, life isn't fair. We have to hold ourselves accountable for our lack of communication skills. Communicate with people in a way that respects all parties involved and in a way that what is being communicated is correctly understood. You are doing yourself and others a disservice by not making sure you are not being offensive to them.

Sometimes, offense happens because we simply don't understand. We lack full knowledge of a situation and we take what we do know and run with it, which allows us to create our own rendition of the situation; which may not even be what the situation is at all. The Bible says to take our ought to our brother (Matthew 18:15). It says to our brother alone. Not to whoever that will listen; not to your friend who will support your pity party stocked full with confetti, horns and balloons. It says to your brother alone, between you and them only, first. Give them the chance to right the wrong. It then says (Matthew 18:16) if he does not take heed then take witnesses with you. Not any kind of witness, but those who you trust to have great discernment to assist you and mediate the issue. Hopefully, that solves the issue because if not, the next step says to take it to the church (Matthew 18:17), make it public.

We tend to shy away from this principal, which becomes a breeding ground for offense. We skip the steps and go straight to tell the world, not just the church, the full story of how we have been wronged. We unconsciously, I think, water the seed of offense by taking hold of it and claiming it for ourselves. "Look at me, they hurt me and I am offended". How about we just be adult enough to handle disagreements when they arise? I'm sure we would have a different outcome if we chose instead to be spiritually sound enough to take our pains and vulnerabilities to our sisters and brothers in hopes of correcting the wrong. We may find that there never should have been a "wrong" in the first place.

Unfortunately, some people, you can't expect to be receptive of what you bring to them. Some people will always be offended and in those situations, you have to take that to the Lord in prayer. Pray for them; that God will take the spirit of offense out of their hearts and replace it with His peace. However, if you are this person, who is easily offended or who holds onto offense, then you have to do more than just pray. You first must pray, but you must also actively work towards change. Ask God to help you put a magnifying glass on yourself so that you can see the deep-rooted things that are causing the offense so that you can do what needs to be done to pluck it out. In doing this, you may stumble upon a gift of discernment to recognize offense in others and become a warrior in the spirit to counter the spirit of offense in their lives. How great would it be for God to use you as defense against the spirit of offense instead of being the individual suffering from the affliction of it?

This is the thing. Offense will not just remain offense. It can and will morph into or invite in other spirits such as bitterness and unforgiveness. These things will fester and grow into many other things. It will become so much harder to release yourself from offense when its cousins join in and start jumping you. This is why we must guard our hearts and minds diligently, daily (Proverbs 4:23). If we allow ourselves to succumb to the wounds inflicted on us by the actions of others, we will end up creating other self-inflicted wounds by allowing the spirit of offense to latch onto us.

So, we have to recognize it as soon as it plants a negative thought in our mind about something someone did or said to us. We have to choose to take the high road in order for us not to end up buried under a tomb that says "here lies a woman or the man full of offense". Is this an easy task, absolutely not. However, it is a worthy one. It will be worth it in the end for you to fight past the flaws of those who offend you. We are all human, none of us have made it until we hear well done, therefore, we will make some mistakes. We will say some things we don't really mean and that we wish we can take back. In those moments, we need to recognize those things for what they are and correct them immediately. It may happen more often than you like; getting offended. However, it is not something you are bound to, unless you want to be. You can move past it. You can come back from the spirit of offense if you take it to God. He is always ready to offer us redemption, if we want it.

Proverbs 19:11 AMP Good sense and discretion make a man slow to anger, and it is his honor and glory to overlook a transgression or an offense (without seeking revenge and harboring resentment).

Leviticus 19:18 AMP "You shall not revenge nor bear any grudge against the sons of your own people, but you shall love your neighbor (acquaintance, associate, companion) as yourself; I am the Lord."

1 Peter 2:23 AMP While being reviled and insulted, He did not revile or insult in return; while suffering, He made no threats of vengeance, but kept entrusting Himself to Him who judges fairly.

Proverbs 18:19 AMP A brother offended is harder to win over than a fortified city, and contentions (separating families) are like the bars of a castle.

Colossians 3:13 AMP Bearing graciously with one another, and willingly forgiving each other if one has a cause for complaint against another; just as the Lord has forgiven you, so should you forgive.

Ephesians 4:32 AMP Be kind and helpful to one another, tenderhearted (compassionate, understanding), forgiving one another (readily and freely), just as God in Christ also forgave you.

Galatians 5:13 AMP For you, my brothers, were called to freedom; only do not let your freedom become an opportunity for the sinful nature (worldliness, selfishness), but through love serve and seek the best for one another.

Ebony L. Brown is a 40-year-old mother of 6, who resides in Louisville, KY with her husband Brisson, her children and a brand-new granddaughter as well. Ebony did not grow up in truth, but from the moment she stepped foot in the doors of Greater Faith Louisville Central, she knew that she was home. Nothing in her life before that moment, had ever given her the peace she had when she first experienced God's touch on that Tuesday night. She works in healthcare, loves decorating, cleaning and is an aspiring interior designer. Ebony is a resilient, prayerful woman of God, who daily strives to be more like Christ in all that she does. Her testimony is still being written, however, what's already in stone will be a huge blessing to other women who find themselves in the same situations as she has. Her birthright is not for sale, she is back where she always belonged, in her Father's House! #ProdiGAL

For all those who have weathered this journey with me, I will be forever grateful for your patience, kindness, and support. At a time when so many others might have turned away, you walked right into the storm with me. At my lowest, your strength, light, and love are what got me through. To my husband, children, mother, and father; thank you for being there with and for me. To my spiritual fathers, thank you. Bishop, who had a vision and seen something special in a forgotten people, I thank you! We exist because you refused to bow to the enemy and staked a claim to the land God promised His people. To my Pastor, who is after God's own heart, thank you for your covering, protection, guidance, and leadership. I'm blessed to be led by you both.

Proverbs 29:18
18 Where there is no vision, the people perish: but he that keepeth the law, happy is he

Jeremiah 3:15
And I will give you pastors according to mine heart, which shall feed you with knowledge and understanding.

Defense is Better Than Offense

"Born of the Water and of the Spirit"

I grew up going to church, and even as a child I would tell my mother that we were missing something. I did not know what it was but I just knew something was not quite right. I was first baptized into the titles Father, Son, and Holy Ghost at 6 years old. I remember being excited to be baptized and when they asked me why, my answer was because I believed in Jesus. I had dreams about God as a little girl, one in particular, Jesus was standing at the top of a case of stairs. There were angels and candles all around. The angels were singing a beautiful song and Jesus said, come to me. Of course, I did not understand at that time but I do believe Jesus was drawing me to Him even then. I am not sure how old I was the first time I dreamed of judgment day, probably around 10 years old. Fire and brimstone rained down from the heavens and I found a big cast Iron skillet to get under and take shelter trying to save myself. I do not quite remember how the dream ended, but what I do know is that God would answer all of my questions and reveal His plan of salvation for me in due time.

As a teenager, I started to notice sin and perversion in the church and I knew we all could and should be living better, I just did not know how. I was full of questions about Jesus and salvation, but even the people at my current church could not give me the answers I was seeking. Eventually I started questioning the trinitarian doctrine; something was off. I was confused and it just did not make sense, but again no one had any straight answers that could satisfy what I was feeling deep within my soul. I would live my life for thirty plus years in darkness, oblivious to what it meant to live in truth. I would not come to the full knowledge and understanding of the truth until the year 2016.

I moved to Atlanta thinking that a geographic change would somehow bring forth an eternal change within me. Foolish me. I fell into the same type of mischief I called myself running away from in the first place. As a matter of fact, it was almost as if it snuck in my carry-on luggage waiting for the right time to pop out and yell "surprise." I tried to run, but it had found me. I went everywhere trying to get my life on track; drug programs, AA meetings, psych wards; you name it, I tried it. I remember one night after a drunken stupor and being discharged from a mental hospital, I lay in my bed crying asking God "where are you, if you're real show me." I grew up believing that all I had to do was profess my faith, believing that Jesus was the son of God and confess that I understood that I was a sinner. That was the remedy of salvation for me all my life. If I did that, then I would be saved. I was accustomed to having ritual religious services, which involved a series of actions being performed, but no true power being exercised.

As much as I knew I wanted to change, I knew I wanted to be a Christian and I knew I wanted to be saved. I did not want to be an addict; I did not want to be depressed and suicidal. I did not want to feel hopeless, but still I had no power to change. I tried with everything in me but my own strength was simply not enough. I found a church there that had pretty good people and good worship services. I remember the Pastor would throw his handkerchief out in the crowd. I wanted to catch one so badly. Like a wide receiver, I would position myself to catch one thinking if he could just throw it my way that I would finally be set free. I was desperate. I watched late night infomercials and ordered prayer cloths but still no change. I tried being baptized again for the second time. I confessed, I believed! What was wrong with me? Maybe, God just simply did not love me? Then one day, as I was scrolling through Facebook, I noticed a high school friend was attending a church back in Louisville. It looked as if she had been changing. Her appearance was different and the way she was speaking about God was refreshing. I remember thinking "wow, she must have really had a true encounter with God." So, I called her up and told her how I had relocated and was trying to live right but struggling. What she said reverberated so loudly in my spirit, I could never forget it. I had never heard this before. "You must be born of the water and the spirit. Water being baptized in Jesus' name and Spirit being filled with the Holy Ghost, evidence by speaking in tongues," she stated matter-of-factly. I didn't fully comprehend what she was saying, but glory to God, I would and soon.

John 3:5-6 KJV
[5] Jesus answered, Verily, verily, I say unto thee, except a man be born of water and of the Spirit, he cannot enter into the kingdom of God. [6] That which is born of the flesh is flesh; and that which is born of the Spirit is spirit.

The baptismal formula was changed from the name of JESUS CHRIST to the words Father, Son, & Holy Ghost by the Catholic Church in the second century. In Acts, we read that Cornelius was a charitable god-fearing man, as good as they came. However, Cornelius and his household were not living according to the plan of salvation. They needed to be saved. God instructed Cornelius on what he had to do in order to be saved. Cornelius sent his men to find Peter, and the Holy Ghost told Peter to go with them. Peter told them about the gospel of Jesus Christ, and Cornelius' whole household was filled with the Holy Ghost and baptized in the name of JESUS. How powerful is that? It is not always that simple when soul-winning, however, it can be. It is our job to take the gospel to the world just as Peter did. It is also our job as recipients of salvation to take heed to the gospel once it is brought to us. That is the only way that the plan for salvation will work for any of us. This is what I wanted. I wanted it not just for myself, but for my entire household, my entire family, to be filled with the spirit of God and baptized in His name. I did not want it to stop there, though. Once I had it, I wanted to share it with the world.

"Desperation"

I was desperate, I know I keep saying this but I need everyone that ever reads these words to understand that things can and will be birthed out of desperation. For instance, the story of the woman with the issue of blood proves how your desperation can draw you closer to God. For twelve years, she bled, suffered, and spent all she had seeing physicians looking for a cure. She was desperate for healing. She felt like an outcast, that no one wanted to be around. She felt like no one cared about her, but when she heard about the power of Christ, great faith welled up inside of her. Great desperation became great determination to be healed. It was relentless within her being. So, when she touched the hem of His garment, Jesus said, "Daughter your faith has healed you." The desperation she was feeling was feeding and fueling her faith to be healed. Jesus is moved by our faith when we connect our faith with the power of God. This, is where I was. This was the fork in the road I had come to and like the woman with the issue of blood I had to make a choice. I was caught between desperation and determination, but not for much longer. My issue would soon be over too.

"Something About the Name JESUS"

Fast-forward, here I am, back in Louisville. I had to go see about this church that had been doing such a drastic change in the life of my old friend from high school. Remember, I was desperate. I was willing to try anything that I could if it meant that I would be set free from the turmoil that plagued me. There was just something about witnessing her change that was telling me that this was worth trying. So, I did. I am so glad that I did.

It was Friends Day. I would never forget that Sunday at church. I was baptized in the only saving name of Jesus Christ. It was absolutely the best thing that ever happened to me. Nothing in my life before that could compare to the feeling I had when I went down in Jesus' name. The feeling is truly indescribable. There really are no words in the English vocabulary that can adequately describe what I felt inside. The Bible says that baptism washes away your sins. I literally felt as if I had been covered in dirt all my life and I was finally clean. Anybody that knows me, knows that this is a big deal. We do not do dirty around these parts. We do not do out of place. We do not do disarray; however, I had been living in disarray for a long time. It was the very first time that I had ever attended an Apostolic church; a multicultural church at that. That was new for me too. I do not have a prejudice bone in my body, but I thought, wow look at all these white people. It was like the Pastor in the pulpit, who was Caucasian, knew exactly what I was thinking. I felt as if he had taken up residence in my mind because immediately, he said, "if you are looking around at all the different races, I hope you don't think heaven is going to be one race. Heaven will be filled with different nationalities." The Pastor preached baptism in a way I'd never heard before. He preached with such authority and conviction. I had never received a word from God like I was receiving it in my spirit that day. Right away, I felt that I needed to obey this preaching. After being baptized, in the only saving name of Jesus, I began to change. Sin just didn't feel right anymore. I was no longer yearning to continue to get high off of my sinful ways. The water that I went down in felt different than the water I was dipped in at 6 and 30 years old. For the first time in my life, I felt lighter and cleansed.

Acts 4:10-12
10 Be it known unto you all, and to all the people of Israel, that by the name of Jesus Christ of Nazareth, whom ye crucified, whom God raised from the dead, even by him doth this man stand here before you whole. 11 This is the stone which was set at nought of you builders, which is become the head of the corner. 12 Neither is there salvation in any other: for there is none other name under heaven given among men, whereby we must be saved.

"Hell Lost Another One"

I will never forget the Tuesday night bible study that changed the trajectory of my entire life. I remember rolling around on the floor like a snake, writhing in discomfort. I remember those demons trembling inside of me, fighting to keep residence where they had been comfortable for decades now. The spirits within me were shaking inside of me as they came face to face with my Pastor. He took dominion and authority, as he called out each of those tormenting spirts by name, one by one. He was not afraid. There was determination in the atmosphere and I remember thinking "today, I will be set free." I felt liberty, boldness, strength, courage, and dominion in the room as he literally warred for my soul. I could feel the fear of them being afraid of eviction, those spirits. They knew their time had come. I was about to be released and set free from the chains they had on me in that very moment. I had never felt anything like this before. "And these signs shall follow them that believe, they shall cast out devils." It was just like we read in the Bible, when those who were demonically possessed would come to Jesus, the disciples, the New Testament church. I had never witnessed anything so powerful in all my life. I was literally witnessing a miracle. I was the miracle. Though afraid, I was relieved. All I knew was, I was tired. Wore out. Done. I was done living that life that had brought me so much pain. I was at wit's end and I was barely holding on, barely gripping the rope that was keeping me from making the choice to end it all. I was done with abuse, addiction, fornication, godlessness; all of it. It was over. No matter how long these spirits had ahold of me, all it took was one encounter with the power of God. I had to let it all go that night. I had to surrender my past in that very moment, in order to have the future that I had always wanted. In order to have the future that God wanted for me. I had to decide then that I wanted to be made whole. That night, Jesus orchestrated a way of escape for me. He sent me to a man of God that would lead me into spiritual deliverance away from the captivity that I had been bound to for far too long. I made the decision, that night, to be free. Chains were broken and my soul surrendered to the awe-inspiring and beautifully amazing power of God on that Tuesday night.

Laying there on that wooden church floor, in spiritual agony, I witnessed him and my church family charge hell for me on that Tuesday night. They went to war for me. I thought I was simply going to a bible study; little did I know I was walking into a battle for my freedom. Victory was awaiting me. I was going to be released from the prison I had been in spiritually for a very long time. Some of these people did not even know me. They did not even know where I lived, how I lived, where I had come from or how I had gotten there, but that did not matter to them. All that mattered to them in that moment was my salvation. It did not matter if I had been high that week, it did not matter if I had laid down with someone that I should not have been laying with, it did not matter whether or not I was living a holy life. For three hours, they prayed for me. Those evil, vile, stubborn spirits did not want to release me, but they had no choice but to let me go. Who can stand against the hand of God? God is a perfect gentleman. He will not force you to choose Him. He will not force you to love Him or live for Him. He will not overpower your will. You will have to choose His will over your own for Him to operate in full capacity in your life. I witnessed the true power of God that night. The power and authority of Jesus Christ, who is God; God in flesh. Hell lost another one! I was finally free. God took back what was rightfully His that night! It is when we are ready that God will set us free. He will not force us to choose freedom. He will offer it to us, but we must make the choice to accept it. By the

power and authority of Jesus Christ, who is God
and God in flesh, that night, hell lost another one.
I was truly FREE! I was and am, free indeed!

James 2:19
19 You believe that God is one; you do well.
Even the demons believe—and tremble!

Mark 16:17
17 And these signs shall follow them that believe;
In my name shall they cast out devils; they shall
speak with new tongue

"Ain't No Party Like a Holy Ghost Party"

I was a worldly partier. I am saying that if there
was drinking, drugging, loud music, ungodly dress,
and ungodly people, I was there. I am so glad that
once I encountered the presence of God, I quickly
realized that what I thought was a party, was not
a party at all. Because in the world, it always
turned into a disaster. The side effects of
"partying like a rock star" always spilled over into
the next day and debilitated me. I remember
waking up most mornings being disgusted with
myself for all the foolish things I had done the
night before. I was tired of being drunk and high, I
was tired of meaningless relationships, and I was
tired of feeling suicidal and hopeless. I was tired

of disappointing my family and tired of my sin. I needed something new, something different. I wanted a change. Right after being baptized, that next weekend, I had met up with a friend to party like we usually did on the weekend. This time was different. I was not able to drink any alcohol, it did not taste the same anymore. I did not have a taste for it. My appetite had changed and I did not even want to consume it. I later learned that this was conviction. I had been convicted by the Holy Spirit. I did not know what was going on at the time, all I knew was that it was not right. I had never felt that way before. I just no longer had any desire to partake in anything that was not pleasing to God. Guess what, it gets better! God was about to blow my mind! He was going to do something supernatural. He was going to fill me with His Spirt, the Holy Ghost, evidence by speaking in tongues. That was another experience that I would never forget. It was in a beautiful Sunday service that I received the baptism of the Holy Ghost. Hands were laid on me and prayer was made. I lost complete control of my tongue; it was an out-of-body experience. It was as if God was right there with me, I could feel His presence near me. I felt such peace and joy in my spirit. The newfound hope I felt was incomparable to anything else that I had ever felt before in my life. I danced, sung, clapped my hands in praise and worship to God. I was in awe of how great and full of love the Lord truly was. The God of the universe knew me and He cared about me, of all people. The Holy Spirit gave me power to overcome sin once and for all. This was the party that I had been looking for, to fill that void I had been living with for all those years. There was no party like this Holy Ghost party and I never wanted it to stop.

Act 1:8
8 But ye shall receive power, after that the Holy Ghost is come upon you: and ye shall be witnesses unto me both in Jerusalem, and in all Judaea, and in Samaria, and unto the uttermost part of the earth.

Acts 2:38
38 Then Peter said unto them, Repent, and be baptized every one of you in the name of Jesus Christ for the remission of sins, and ye shall receive the gift of the Holy Ghost.

SO HOW DID I GET HERE, WHAT HAPPENED? I became a ProdiGAL!

"Offense"

I was offended! The spirit of offense is a beast. It carries so many debilitating side effects with it. With offense, came blindness and anger. When I became offended, I became blind. Offense shifts your vision and instead of being focused on your purpose, you are focusing solely on offense. If the enemy can steal your vision, then he can kill your purpose. Offended people become too hard hearted to hear God's voice. The enemy uses offense to destroy lives. It is like a cancer, a terminal illness that threatens your sanity and then your entire being. It invaded me and took over my feelings and emotions. It brought with it, it's cousins, resentment and bitterness. A brutal assault ensued against my mind, my body, my faith, and everything that I had come to believe because I allowed myself to be offended. I was offended and angry with God and His body for unanswered prayers that I had been believing to come to past. I often charged God for the mistakes of others. I charged God with the humanness of His people, though I knew He was blameless. I treated others as if I, myself, was without flesh and they were the only ones with flaws because all I knew in that season was, I was offended and it was everybody's fault, but mine. I became ungrateful and impatient. Instead of looking at all the many things God had done, I focused on what He had not done. I became weary in well-doing. I disconnected and isolated, I became bored and lonely. Let me stop right here and give you a bit of advice, this is never the right thing to do. Isolation is the stomping ground of the enemy. If he can get you alone, he knows that he has more chance at victory because one can set a thousand, two, ten thousand. So, how many more could a whole congregation of believers set to flight? Loneliness too. It is a monster as well. This world is full of spirits and if we do not guard ourselves from them, we will not make it. They will overtake us and snuff out any promise that God has given to us. Loneliness will have us in places we would never visit, with people we would not ordinarily engage with and doing things we would never do. The closer we are to God, the further we are from our flesh. It is of the utmost importance that we truly keep our relationship with God at the forefront of our lives so that we do not allow things such as offense or loneliness to cost us our birthright. The enemy will stop at nothing, to gain your soul. You must stand firm against all adversity and not allow that to happen.

Okay, now that our little commercial break is over, back to the story. I did not want to talk to God or anyone that I knew who had a true relationship with Him because I did not want to feel conviction. I became delusional. I saw what I wanted to see and heard what I wanted to hear. It did not matter if it was the truth or not. To be spiritually blind, is a death sentence.

When I was dealing with the spirit of offense, or maybe I should say when I decided to allow offense to become more important than my relationship with God, I had to come to the realization of some things in order to be set free from it. One of the most important things that I had to come to grips with was the fact that I had the power. I had to understand that I should have never allowed someone else's misrepresentation of Christ to affect my relationship with Him. The truth of the matter is that sometimes people blatantly and intentionally misrepresent God. Other times, they ignorantly and unintentionally misrepresent Him. Therefore, we must guard our hearts. Our relationship with God should always remain solid enough so that no matter what anyone around us or the enemy might place in our path, we are able to overcome it because we have God on our side. However, that did not happen with me. Offense overpowered my thinking and I just could not even see my hand right in front of my face, nevertheless anything else. Nothing was right in the world anymore.

The body of Christ is made up of many different parts, people, nationalities, backgrounds, and attitudes. It is important to remember that like me, everyone is a work in progress. We are not saved, until we receive well done. The church is made up of people with flaws, who make mistakes, but strive daily to be more like Christ. When I was dealing with the spirit of offense, it was most important that I realized that it was solely my responsibility to overcome offense. No one else's, strictly mine.

Proverbs 18:19
19 A brother offended is more unyielding than a strong city, and quarreling is like the bars of a castle.

Hebrew 13:5
5 Let your manner of living be without covetousness, and be content with such things as ye have. For He hath said, "I will never leave thee, nor forsake thee";

Galatians 6:9
9 And let us not be weary in well doing: for in due

season we shall reap, if we faint not

"Prayer Life < A Life of Prayer"

I lost the desire to pray. I lost connection and intimacy with God. With a lack of prayer, you will start to make poor decisions. You will be unable to hear the voice of God, because prayer is how we commune with Him. You relinquish all power to the enemy and give him full opportunity to attack. It is open season on your spirit.

A life of prayer requires effort, discipline, and consistency. Instead of viewing prayer as a routine, with no meaning, we must view prayer as a privilege. We are blessed with the awesome ability to connect and commune with God, the creator of the universe; your Father who has all power, wisdom, and authority! Prayer should be the foundation of our relationship with Jesus. Prayer moves the hand of God. It changes us inwardly, and changes our situations. Prayer has the power to change your course to get you back onto the path that God has destined for you from before your birth. A life of prayer is and must be a choice and a lifestyle.

Luke 21:36

36 Watch ye therefore, and pray always, that ye may be accounted worthy to escape all these things that shall come to pass, and to stand before the Son of man.

Colossians 4:2
2 Continue in prayer, and watch in the same with thanksgiving;

"Struggling to Forgive"

Three things that helped me forgive.

Humbleness.

Prayer.

Acceptance.

Sometimes we struggle to forgive because of unresolved pains and hurts. It could be things that have happened in our childhood, our upbringings, or generational curses. Forgiving takes determination and willingness to change and please God. Forgiveness is not always easy; it is easier to forgive when you humbly extend as much grace to the person who you need to forgive as you want Jesus to extend to you.

Prayer is the answer to forgiveness. Pray, pray, pray, pray, and pray some more. Ask God to heal your mind and heart to remove the pain and desire for revenge. Yes, I said it. I can only be real. Our flesh sometimes forgets that vengeance is not ours and we want to take matters into our own hands and replace God as if we have the authority to do so. We do not have that type of authority. Therefore, we must pray in the spirit. With much prayer, Jesus will help you change your attitude towards people and situations and help you overcome resentment. Accept people as they are, accept that the person you need to forgive may never ask for forgiveness. Accept that the people you need to forgive you, may never accept your apology, and offer you forgiveness. Just know, you did your part. Forgiveness is not just for them, but for you. When you forgive, it releases happiness and freedom. When I was struggling with offense, I had too much pride to forgive and we all know that pride is what comes before the fall.

Matthew 6:14-15
14 For if ye forgive men their trespasses, your heavenly Father will also forgive you:
15 But if ye forgive not men their trespasses, neither will your Father forgive your trespasses.

Ephesians 4:32
32 Be kind and compassionate to one another, forgiving each other, just as in Christ God forgave you.

"Backsliding"

Backsliding; a term used within Christianity to describe a process by which an individual who has converted to Christianity reverts to pre-conversion habits and falls into sin; when a person turns from God to pursue their own desire. Backsliding started in my heart. My heart was hardened toward the things of God. God knows our heart. I know people tend to throw that term around loosely, but it is true. He really does know our heart. The Bible says, the heart is deceitful above all things, and desperately wicked; who can know it? You may be able to fool everyone around you, but you cannot fool God! I left God mentally before I ever physically left the church. It did not happen overnight. It crept in slowly. I could feel me pulling back, I could feel the resistance. Backsliding was a decision I made, a decision to deliberately walk away from God. It could have been prevented. I had the power through the Holy Spirit to overcome backsliding. It was not that the Holy Spirit lost its power to sustain me. It was my rebellion and disobedience that allowed me to be deceived by the pleasures of sin. Be aware of the enemy's tactics, such as lust, offense, and carnality. If you find yourself slipping backwards, stop and examine yourself. Make time with God! Live a life of prayer. Allow correction from your spiritual leaders. If you believe they are supposed to be the watchman on the wall for your soul, then you should trust their voice in your life. Trust their warning, their urgency, and their direction for your life. Engage in fellowship. Do not let the enemy make you believe that you can get through anything alone. Find you some true friends that do not mind warring with you. Reach out to them. Share your burdens with the ones that you know will stand in the gap for your soul. A backslidden state is a miserable place to be in. I was lifeless, broken, empty and full of shame.

Hosea 14:4
4 I will heal their backsliding, I will love them freely: for mine anger is turned away from him.

Jeremiah 8:5
5 Why then has this people turned away in perpetual backsliding? They hold fast to deceit; they refuse to return.

"Jesus is at the Well"

The living water from Christ brings, peace, joy, and everlasting life. Jesus' promise to the woman at the well is for all His children who are obedient. It is a promise that, if we drink the gospel of Jesus Christ, He will cleanse and purify us externally and give us eternal life. Jesus extends love, compassion, and grace to us all, regardless of our past, flaws and failures, just like He did for the woman at the well. This story examples that only Jesus can satisfy and quench our thirsts. We must be totally dependent on Jesus and drink from His spiritual well every day of our lives.

John 4:14 AMP
14 But whoever drinks the water that I give him will never be thirsty again. But the water that I give him will become in him a spring of water [satisfying his thirst for God] welling up [continually flowing, bubbling within him] to eternal life."

John 7:37-38 AMP
37 Now on the last and most important day of the feast, Jesus stood and called out [in a loud voice], "If anyone is thirsty, let him come to Me and drink! 38 He who believes in Me [who adheres to, trusts in, and relies on Me], as the

Scripture has said, 'From his innermost being will flow continually rivers of living water.'"

"Nothing but the Blood"

God paid the ransom and provided the sacrifice with the precious blood of Jesus (who was God in flesh), for the debt we owed to Him for our sins. The mosaic law required the blood of animals to be offered for sins, however, their blood was not sufficient. So, once a year, they sacrificed animals over and over. Jesus was the ultimate sacrifice, there was no more need for the blood of animals. Jesus paid the price, once and for all. Without the shedding of blood, there would be no forgiveness. The blood of Jesus obtained eternal redemption for us.

Being covered by the blood of Jesus ensures life and protection just like when God required the Israelites to paint the blood, they collected from the Passover lamb, on the doorposts and lintels. Those who were obedient and had applied the blood of the Passover lamb were protected.

Jesus has the power to heal. Christ took on brutal punishment for humanity. He suffered during His death and His suffering purchased our healing. The Bible tells us that by His stripes we are healed.

The blood makes it possible for us to overcome any situation. It has not lost its power. And it never will. The power of the blood of Jesus has provided everything you need to live a life of victory.

Ephesians 1:7
7 In him we have redemption through his blood, the forgiveness of sins, in accordance with the riches of God's grace

Hebrews 9:14
14 How much more, then, will the blood of Christ, who through the eternal Spirit offered himself unblemished to God, cleanse our consciences from acts that lead to death, so that we may serve the living God!

Isaiah 53:5
5 But he was wounded for our transgressions, he was bruised for our iniquities: the chastisement of our peace was upon him; and with his stripes we are healed

"Condemnation"

Condemnation is from the devil, but conviction is from God. Conviction leads you closer to God and to repentance; while condemnation leads you further away. Condemnation feels like guilt, discouragement, heaviness, and hopelessness. It paralyzes you and keeps you from being able to let go of your past sin. Condemnation has no liberty; it killed my praise and worship and made it impossible for me to receive anything from God. Shame and condemnation revealed my sin. Your sin will always find you out and take you further than you want to go. Break free from condemnation. Know that Jesus loves you and that He is gracious and merciful. He will not and does not condemn us.

Romans 8:1
1 There is therefore now no condemnation to them which are in Christ Jesus, who walk not after the flesh, but after the spirit

"Letting Go of Shame"

First, you must identify what shame is. A painful feeling of humiliation or distress caused by the consciousness of wrong or foolish behavior. Let go of shameful behaviors. Repent and pray for forgiveness and then believe that you are forgiven. Forgive yourself. I believe that one of the hardest things for any of us to do is to forgive ourselves. I do not know why it is so hard to give ourselves another chance. We are always our own worse critics. I am telling you that it is a must that you also forgive you too. Move on and do better. We cannot change the past; however, we are equipped with everything we need to change our future. Do what is approved by God. Do all that you know is right and allow God to renew your mind every single day.

2 Timothy 2:15 AMP
15 Study and do your best to present yourself to God approved, a workman [tested by trial] who has no reason to be ashamed, accurately handling and skillfully teaching the word of truth.

"Good Company"

When trying to come back from backsliding, it is very important to surround yourself with those of like faith that want to see you win. While we do need friendships that hold us accountable, we also need friends who add strength and encouragement. A godly friend will speak truth into your life, even if you do not want to hear it. A godly friend will help you keep focus and stay on track. You must trust that they are speaking to you in a spirit of love. You must give them the authority to say "now you know", even when you really want them to condone your mess. A godly friend is worth more than a worldly one, any day of the week.

Proverbs 27:9 NLT
9 The heartfelt counsel of a friend is as sweet as perfume and incense.

Proverbs 27:17 KJV
17 Iron sharpeneth iron; so, a man sharpeneth the countenance of his friend.

"Keep Your Mouth Off My Children"

I heard this plain as day. This is what the Lord said to me at a night service while I was praying for Jesus to heal my heart of bitterness and disdain for those who had hurt me. A healthy part of healing is learning not to want to hurt others the way they have hurt you, whether that is verbally, physically, mentally, or spiritually. I do not think we realize the damage we can do to one's spiritual walk with our unruly tongues. As soon as the enemy reminds you of what was done to you, cast it out of your mind immediately. Give it no attention. Do not even speak on it. Lay it at the altar and leave it there. You will be much better off allowing vengeance to be God's, because it is supposed to be His anyway. Stop rehashing old wounds. It is like pulling scabs off sores that are trying to heal. While it may eventually heal, it will leave a scar there as a reminder of who you once were. The healing process begins when you stop blaming others. Be fully healed and stay fully healed!

Ephesians 4:29 KJV
29 Let no corrupt communication proceed out of your mouth, but that which is good to the use of edifying, that it may minister grace unto the hearers.

Proverbs 15:28 KJV
28 The heart of the righteous studieth to answer: but the mouth of the wicked poureth out evil things.

"The Posture of Prayer"

Each of us must have a repentant heart when asking for forgiveness. It is okay to be broken and desperate, to weep even. Rent your heart. Show the Lord that you have deep sorrow. For the kind of sorrow God wants us to experience leads us away from sin and results in salvation. There is no regret for that kind of sorrow. But worldly sorrow, which lacks repentance, results in spiritual death.

Joel 2:12-13 AMP
12 "Even now," says the LORD, "Turn and come to Me with all your heart [in genuine repentance], with fasting and weeping and mourning [until every barrier is removed and broken fellowship is restored]; 13 Rip your heart to pieces [in sorrow and contrition] and not your garments." Now return [in repentance] to the LORD your God, For He is gracious and compassionate, slow to anger, abounding in lovingkindness [faithful to His covenant with His people]; and He relents [His sentence of] evil [when His people genuinely repent].

"Smite the Enemy"

When fighting spiritual battles, we must understand that they cannot be fought in the flesh. They can only be won spiritually. In order to kill all my sinful habits, I had to relearn to fight in the spirit. While God was willing to help me fight, there were some battles that I had to conquer and totally destroy in order to be free again. Be careful letting things live that God has told you to kill. It will come back to destroy you. It will cost you your position in the Kingdom of God and the anointing God wants to give to you. The Lord gave King Saul specific instructions on how to handle a battle. God told Saul to go and smite Amalek, and utterly destroy all that they have, and spare them not; but slay both man and woman, infant and suckling, ox and sheep, camel and donkey. The Amalekites attack Israel first in Exodus and several times throughout the Old Testament. Amalekites were always at war with Israel and with God. Because of Saul's rebellion and disobedience, the Amalekites continued to be the enemy of Israel for over hundreds of years. Haman, a descendant from the Amalekite king known as Agag, planned to destroy the Jews in the book of Esther. However, God turned it around and used Esther to save the Jews. Haman, his sons, and the rest of Israel's enemies were destroyed. Partial obedience is complete disobedience and the Bible says that obedience is better than sacrifice. Smite your enemy and utterly destroy all that wages war with God.

Samuel 15:22-23
22 And Samuel said, Hath the Lord as great delight in burnt offerings and sacrifices, as in obeying the voice of the Lord? Behold, to obey is better than sacrifice, and to hearken than the fat of rams.

23 For rebellion is as the sin of witchcraft, and stubbornness is as iniquity and idolatry. Because thou hast rejected the word of the Lord, he hath also rejected thee from being king.

"Koinonia"

Fellowship. Koinonia is also translated as fellowship. It comes from a root word that means "partner" or "companion." It has in it the idea of "sharing"—sharing possessions, sharing experiences, sharing life, sharing one's self with another. Fellowship with and stay connected to the body of Christ. Being an introvert has been one of my biggest struggles. Introverts prefer being alone or around a few people and they avoid crowds. Let God transform you even beyond where you were before. Allow God to give you some extrovert qualities to go with your introverted personality. Be bigger. Be greater. Be healed.

Life is not perfect. You must let yourself grow. Do not spend your life avoiding people or sweating differences of personalities, comments, likes or dislikes. Life is bigger than that. Love God. Love people. The alternative is just staying stuck your whole life. Do not be that person. Those people that seclude themselves and think they have it made are not being real with themselves. They are just miserable and limiting their lives. Break the habit of being by yourself. Habits are ways of behaving or a tendency that someone has settled into. I had to step out of my comfort zone. The more you do uncomfortable things the more comfortable it becomes. This is where we grow. Be intentional about connecting with the body of Christ. It will help save your life.

Hebrews 10:24-25
And let us consider how we may spur one another on toward love and good deeds, not giving up meeting together, as some are in the habit of doing, but encouraging one another—and all the more as you see the Day approaching.

1 John 1:7

7 But if we walk in the light, (A) as he is in the light, we have fellowship with one another, and the blood of Jesus, his Son, purifies us from all sin

"ATTITUDE"

I will never forget this dream I had where I was standing in a desert. The soil was brown, cracked, and dry and my feet was embedded into the dirt, as if I was planted in the ground. I was standing there looking at my feet, when a Prophet called my name. This prophet is great friends with my Bishop, he comes to minister to the church I belong to often. Ebony, he said with a voice of authority, come out of that attitude! Immediately, a massive hand reached down and pulled me up out of the ground. It sounded like pulling weeds from the root. My feet were stuck, set on solid ground. My interpretation of this dream was God would lift me out of calamity and establish my steps, but I would have to allow Him to uproot those things that were not like Him. I had to change my attitude. Attitude is a settled way of thinking or feeling about someone or something; typically, one that is reflected in a person's behavior. Having the right attitude is everything. A positive attitude helps avoid negative thinking. Attitude is a result of upbringing and experiences. When you change your attitude, you change your prospective and outlook on life. Replace negative thoughts with positive ones. My father always told me 90% of everything is attitude and 10% is what happens to us. **ATTITUDE** is a choice. Put on Jesus's attitude, bear the fruit of the Spirit. These are the attributes that should be evident in a Christian.

Galatians 5:22-23 KJV
22 But the fruit of the Spirit is love, joy, peace, patience, kindness, goodness, faithfulness, gentleness, self-control; against such things there is no law.

"God's Plan VS My Plan"

God is sovereign, supreme, and has all power. I was arrogant and full of idolatry
to think I knew more than God. He will not force us to do anything. I allowed myself to believe this huge lie, that my plan would be better for my life, when Jesus' plan is always greater. It is comforting to know that God has everything in control and He already knows the plans that He

has for us. God does not need our help or our opinions. God's will, is for the advancement of His kingdom. It is important for us to trust God's plan even when it does not align with our own. Being in the will of God is the happiest, healthiest, and safest place to be. You have free will to step out of the will of God, but we are not free from the consequences of such decisions.

"For I know the plans I have for you," declares the Lord, "plans to prosper you and not to harm you, plans to give you a hope and a future. " — Jeremiah 29:11

"Get Your Praise Back"

The enemy would love to steal and still your praise. One means that he completely takes it away, the other means that he just causes you not to move. It means that you will sit down on your praise, even when you feel it bubbling up inside of you. Do not allow the enemy to do either to you. Why? Because praise is powerful! Your praise is a weapon against the enemy. When praise goes up, blessings come down. Praise glorifies God and shifts your focus from the problem to the problem solver. When you magnify God, your situation becomes smaller and it serves as a reminder that God is in control. Praise ushers in the Spirit of

God and releases strength and faith. Praise God in His sanctuary; praise Him in His mighty heavens. Praise Him for His acts of power; praise Him for His surpassing greatness. Praise Him with the clash of cymbals, praise Him with resounding cymbals. Let everything that has breath, praise the LORD. Psalm 150

"Sold My Birthright"

I felt I sold my position in the Kingdom of God and my inheritance. God's plans for my life had been put on an auction block and the enemy was there to purchase them. If you are worried you sold your birthright, it is not too late to turn back to God and turn away from sin. God still has a plan for you. You did not destroy His plan, it may be delayed, but it is not destroyed! God's love is waiting for a repentant sinner to come to his senses. He is waiting with open arms to receive you. Trust Jesus. Be confident that God will restore you. Trust that our Father, yours and mine, still has good plans for your life. Turn back to God. Pray, seek, fast. What the devil meant for evil, God will turn it around and use it for His good.

Philippians 1:6 KJV
6 being confident of this very thing, that he which
hath begun a good work in you will perform it
until the day of Jesus Christ:

Be **COMMITTED** and stay **CONSISTENT**!
CONTRIBUTE TO THE KINGDOM OF GOD! Ask
what can you do to help in your church? Be a
prayer warrior, a worshipper, teach a Bible study.
Give of your time, talents, and treasures. What
can you be responsible for? Hone your natural
and spiritual skills, discover your gifts. Allow God
to reveal your ministry unto you. Once He has
revealed it to you, perform that ministry unto the
Lord! Not to a person, not to people, but to God.
Win souls! Tell everyone you know about the
goodness of Jesus and all that He has done for
you! Commit your way to the Lord; trust in Him,
and He will act." (Psalm 37:5)

"The Word is the Best Teacher"

God speaks to us through the Bible. He reveals
Himself. He teaches us what is acceptable and
what is unacceptable. Whatever you may be
struggling with, can be found in His word. A
solution is there. The Word of God helps us build

our relationship with Jesus. It helps build our character. When reading the Word of God, we gain wisdom, renew our minds and grow from faith to faith as we learn His doctrine.

Timothy 3:16-17
16 All scripture is given by inspiration of God, and is profitable for doctrine, for reproof, for correction, for instruction in righteousness:
17 That the man of God may be perfect, thoroughly furnished unto all good works.

"Get Back to Your Father's House"

The peace and joy that came from my relationship with Jesus was incomparable. There was a calmness and confidence regardless of life's situations or circumstances. Being with Him, in His Presence, and with other believers is definitely worth facing any shame, fear, wounds, scars or consequences. Take back your birthright! Fight for your position in God's kingdom. Your Father is full of compassion. He has a robe of mercy and grace waiting to welcome you home. He has a ring of affection, waiting for you. Your father is well-heeled, your shoes are waiting. Come out of the field, climb out of the filth of the mud within that pigpen that you stayed far too long in with the swine. There is no need to eat husks, eat of the fatted calf. Remember ProdiGAL, when you return, you will not return to rags, you will return to the riches that your Father has laid up specifically for you. Come to your senses and get back to your Father's house. I promise you that He is waiting. It pains me to admit that I once left my Fathers' house. However, it excites me and blesses me to get to rejoice and celebrate my return. I am a ProdiGAL!

Zachariah 1:3 Return to me,' declares the Lord Almighty, 'and I will return to you,' says the Lord Almighty.

Grief:

Deep sorrow, especially that caused by someone's death.

Grief is a natural response to loss. It is usually the emotion that immediately comes to us when something or someone we love passes away. Often, the emotional suffering that comes with death can become extremely overwhelming for us. Grief comes with unexpected emotions. I know that when I lost my nephew in a motorcycle accident several years ago, I was absolutely overwhelmed. I had never felt such deep emotions before in my life. One minute you could be fine, the next, tears would be steadily streaming down your face that you are completely unable to stop. These unexpected emotions usually come from shock, anger, disbelief, profound sadness and sometimes even guilt. We guilt ourselves into thinking we could have changed something; we could have done more to change the situation. The truth of the matter though, is usually that we couldn't have. However, we beat ourselves up about it and it only causes us to experience more grief and despair. Though it is hard, when grieving, we have to learn to forgive ourselves for the things we never did or said or wanted to do or say before our loved one was ripped from our lives for eternity. If we don't, the grief will eat us alive from the inside out.

It's such a sorrowful place. Grief. It can become dark and relentless if we don't find a place to get our footing. It doesn't just come with death but it also comes with any sort of desensitizing loss, such as divorce. I remember when I first got divorced, it was one of the most painful times in my life. I was devastated. I had believed that God was going to heal my marriage. It was tumultuous and depressing for more years than not and I still felt as if I was experiencing a living death when I came to the realization of what signing those papers would truly mean for the rest of my life. We argued more than we laughed, we avoided each other more than we enjoyed one another's company and we said mean things more than we complimented one another. However, I spent my entire youth in that relationship so losing it really broke my heart. Heartbreak is definitely a side effect of grief. Or is grief a side effect of heartbreak? I'm not sure. All I know is that they both are very painful and unfortunately, they are a part of living.

This is what we need to come to the realization of. Grief is usually associated with death in some form. We have to find the silver lining and find the life within it. We have to remind ourselves of what it means to continue to live even when death is trying its best to suffocate us.

Grief forces us to try to balance our feelings of pain and loss all while still moving forward. Too often we aren't honest about our emotions and our mental state when it comes to grieving. Sometimes our lives require us to continue to keep going even when we might need to take a pause to actually allow ourselves to experience the grief. The pain of it challenges us not to deal with it, but if we don't, it will show up later in a place we don't want it to rear its ugly head.

There is a place we can turn to though; the scripture. The word of God is there to not only guide us and direct our paths but to also comfort us and ease the pain that is associated with any type of grief that we find ourselves experiencing.

God said that He would never put more on us than we can bare, (1 Corinthians 10:13). However, what we need to understand in this is that He will show up to handle what we can't. He may not take away the strain of the burden, but He will step in and carry what we cannot. Give your grief to God, He is able to carry it.

John 16:22 So, with you: Now is your time of grief, but I will see you again and you will rejoice, and no one will take away your joy.

Romans 8:18 I consider that our present sufferings are not worth comparing with the glory that will be revealed in us.

Psalms 34:18 The Lord is close to the brokenhearted and saves those who are crushed in spirit.

Matthew 11:28-30 Come to me, all you who are weary and burdened, and I will give you rest. Take my yoke upon you and learn from me, for I am gentle and humble in heart, and you will find rest for your souls. For my yoke is easy and my burden is light.

Katherine Grimes is a 45-year-old woman of God who currently resides in North Carolina. She was born in Michigan. She is the mother of twin girls Madison and Lauren, who left this life before her, and she misses them deeply every day.

Family is very important to her. Her sister, Kendra, is her best friend. She has been with her through many storms.

Her friends affectionately call her Kat. She has such a witty disposition and can come up with a hashtag for any situation at the drop of a hat.

Kat loves animals. She currently has several dogs, cats, chickens, and goats living on her property.

She believes in the power of God because He has shown up so mightily in her life numerous times. Even through heartbreak, trials, and tribulations, He somehow always ends up showing up to let her know He is there.

Her favorite things to do are to be with her family, visit her friends, and go on road trips. She recently took a two-week trip across the United States, visiting several tourist sites (including the Grand Canyon), staying in hotels on some stops, and camping outdoors at others. She is adventurous and loves to be wherever there is love and laughter.

One of her favorite worship songs is I Still Believe by Jeremy Camp because it has gotten her through some of the most challenging times in her life. Her favorite scripture is Psalms 27:14.

The one thing she wants people to gather from her chapter the most is to trust in God. No matter how a situation looks, no matter how hard it is to keep your faith and trust Him or how it turns out, know that He is always working every situation in your life to turn for your good. Even when it seems impossible, He will make the impossible happen. God will use your brokenness to minister to others. Get to know God, love God, and trust God in all that you do.

Good Grief!

Grief: is something we all know about but pray we never have to experience intimately. My journey with grief began at the age of 21. My life was barely even getting started, and here I was, a single mother of two beautiful twin girls. It was December 1998, the girls' first Christmas, and what should have been a joyous time most assuredly was not. It was far from the case. I had traveled to my parent's house in Virginia Beach so they could partake in the girls' first Christmas. I wanted to be close to family. Christmas is always the season for that.

We sat around and talked on Christmas Day and planned what we would do the following day. Well, as life would have it, our plans didn't go as planned. Isn't that something? How we prepare for some things, but what we prepare for is not always what comes to pass. Such was the case this year. Those plans we made that day, never happened.

Lauren, the baby of the two, who was bigger than her older sister, woke up the day after Christmas crying. I did all the typical mommy things, changed her, held her, and tried to feed her, yet nothing worked. I had tried everything I knew to do to soothe a crying baby.

None of those things seem to be able to do the job. So, what do you think I did next? I was home with my parents; therefore, someone who had done this before was there.

I decided to go and wake my mom.

After waking my mom and seeing that she was awake enough not just to hear but understand what I was telling her, I let her know that I had been unsuccessful with calming Lauren, and I needed her assistance with getting her to stop crying. My mother got up and attempted to do all she could to calm Lauren as well. To no avail, her attempts to console her seemed as if it was also in vain. The crying went on for what seemed like hours. I made a phone call to her NICU nurse, who said trust your motherly instincts. I felt as if I would never have a chance. My instincts were screaming, something is wrong, take her now.

She began puking as I prepared to pick her up and take her to the hospital. After she was done vomiting, she turned this ghastly color. I immediately stopped preparing to go to the hospital on my own. Instead, I picked the phone back up and called 911. The first responding officers were there in minutes, and the ambulance arrived almost immediately behind them. The paramedic swooped her up and said we must go now. I hurried out of the house and into the back of the ambulance with my beautiful girl. I don't think I fully grasped what was going on as I rode in the ambulance. Nor, did I realize the direness of the situation at that moment. I thought she was sick with a virus, had colic, or something of that nature. I would soon find out, that was not the case. It was a very short trip since my mom only lived a few miles away. It only took us about 5 minutes to arrive at the hospital. Still, it was the most eerily short, deathly quiet ambulance ride you could imagine. Once out of the ambulance and into the hospital, everything was a blur.

I don't even recall all the events that took place while we were there. The one thing I remember is hearing the doctor say that Lauren was breathing on her own, but he was unsure of what happened or how much damage occurred during that time. He said that she would be transferred to the Children's Hospital as she would receive better care there because, of course, they specialized in pediatric care.

The ambulance transported us to Children's Hospital. I felt so numb on the ride there. I didn't know what was going on. However, I just knew my baby would be okay.

When I arrived at the Children's Hospital, they accused me of shaking my Lauren. I, the one person who loved her more than I loved myself. I would never do such a thing, anything, to hurt either of my girls.

They were an extension of my own life.

Both of them had become my lungs when they were born. I was breathing every day because of their existence. It broke my heart that they would conjure up this horrible accusation against me because of their inability to pinpoint how she was experiencing brain swelling. Hearing someone believe I could or would harm my child was heart-wrenching. In transparency, I was so angry that I had to leave the room because all I could think about was punching this woman in the face right there in the middle of that room. How could she say those gross things about me? I mean, I really wanted to, but I didn't. That would only cause me to look guilty. I had to leave the room to release the emotions quickly building within me.

The next few days were filled with tests and evaluations. I never once listened to the reports of those doctors. They were simply practicing medicine. I knew that God had all power in this situation, and I just knew the Lord would heal my baby, and when He did, I would be able to take her home and watch her grow into a beautiful young woman. I would be able to watch her graduate high school and college if she chose to go.

I would be able to watch her change the world one day with her contribution to it. I would see her marry the love of her life and birth babies of her own. I would be Nana, Granny, or Mamaw to those same babies. My faith during those days was the strongest it had ever been. I would not allow it to be shaken. I just couldn't. Lauren needed me to stand on God's word and trust Him for her sake.

So, I refused to allow it to waver.

I truly believed God would perform a miracle. I knew that Lauren would be another victory, another testimony for others to hear and know that God was all-powerful! Until I decided to slip out and attend a local church. Something happened in that service, and I felt a loss. I don't know how or why, but I knew my baby wasn't coming home with me at that moment. Something in my spirit just told me that everything I thought would never happen would indeed happen. Do you remember me mentioning earlier in this chapter that plans don't always go as planned? Well, this was no different.

This I was not prepared for. I returned to the hospital heavy and broken in my spirit, but I tried my best to carry on as I had before. I tried, but I believe others sensed the change in me. I believe it was the very next day that the doctor came and sat us down. We were informed that there was no brain activity and that she would never be more than what she currently was at that moment.

How? Why? I had so many questions. I was immediately filled with the most tremendous grief I've ever known. She was just a baby. My baby. How could this happen to my baby?

At twenty-one years of age, I would be placed in the most unfortunate position and be forced to decide between allowing machines to keep my baby alive or letting her go. I chose peace. I chose safety in the arms of Jesus where she could be free instead of here connected to these whirling machines. It was the single hardest decision I had ever made thus far. As I sat in a dark room watching my precious 10-week-old baby take her final breaths, my heart was broken, my faith was destroyed, and my spirit was crushed. I had no idea how I would possibly be able to get up from here. In those moments, I began to question all the things I would have, could have, or should have done differently that may have led to a different outcome. If I had only known, I would have done something to change this outcome. Surely, I could have done something. If I had only known, I wouldn't be standing there at that precise moment with this as my fate. Sadly, those very thoughts would haunt me for many years to come.

That single moment would also define how I would mother her twin sister, Madison. While Madison was the oldest of the girls, she was also the smallest, as I stated before. She weighed just over 2 lbs. when she was born and overcame many obstacles as an infant. And yet no matter how hard she worked to show me and others that she was a fighter, there was still a lingering fear inside me that would not allow me to become close to her. What if I lost her too? I couldn't stand the thought of experiencing the same heartbreak. I did not want to ever experience the grief of losing a child. No mother wants that.

As the years began to pass, that mindset quickly faded, and I began to soak up every moment with Madison, cherishing each as a blessing from above. She was and still is my beautiful mini-me. We quickly became inseparable. In fact, many would often comment that she was my shadow. I knew it was meant as slander, but I did not care. She was my whole world. Nothing and no one mattered more than she did.

And while time moved on quickly, the fear of losing her remained in my mind's depths. That fear would one day become a reality. At just seventeen years old, my daughter began her day as she did most, listening to praise music and worshiping the Lord as she got ready for school and work. It should have been a typical run-of-the-mill day. However, that would not be the case. Again, plans somehow seemed to go awry.

As I wrapped up subbing for my first class of the day, I glanced down at my phone and saw several missed calls, texts, and voicemails. As I listened to my husband's voice, my heart stopped. "It's Madison. You need to come home now. Please hurry."

As I struggled to comprehend what was going on, I looked at the faces of the high schoolers in that classroom and simply said, "I need to leave. Please be responsible and get to your next class." I grabbed my things and ran down the various hallways towards the exit of the building. As I entered the final hallway before exiting the building, I could see the substitute coordinator approaching. I mumbled, "I am sorry, my daughter, I have to leave now. I am so sorry," as I continued running past him. I often wonder what went through that gentleman's mind that day as a frantic mom ran past him, not even taking the time to explain the entire situation. Yet, I remember him saying, "go, just go, don't stop, I will take care of everything." I wonder if he had ever experienced that scenario before or if he has since then. I pray not. No one should.

As I drove like a maniac on the road to get home, many thoughts flooded my mind. I was unprepared for what I saw as I flew up my driveway. My daughter lay lifeless on a stretcher. Two paramedics were about to place her in the back of the ambulance. As another paramedic approached, he informed me she was breathing, but she still was not responding. Everything else seemed like a blur. I remember falling into my husband's arms, trying desperately to wrap my mind around everything. Eternity flashed before me in a moment, and I looked at him and asked, "She will go to Heaven, right? I know not everyone that dies makes it to Heaven, but she will, won't she?" At that moment, it was all that mattered. Had I done enough to ensure that her eternity would be spent praising Jesus and not in torment with the demons in hell? His response still resonates with me, "there is no doubt in my mind, she will make it." I would not find comfort in that statement for years to come.

We hurriedly grabbed things from the house and rushed to the hospital, making phone calls on the way. I had to call all three of her jobs and let them know she would not be coming in. I made calls to her Pastor and family members, desperately asking them to pray and have all others join in with prayers. I needed everyone to stop and touch the face of God on her behalf and my own. It was just a short drive to the hospital, yet it seemed like it took forever to get there. Again, I was numb. I was ushered into a room where I waited for the doctor. Her words were, we do not know the extent of the damage. It does not look good. We will need to transfer her to the Children's Hospital. If you are a praying person and believe in miracles, you need to pray for one right now. I had never heard those words from a doctor before, and honestly, I wasn't sure if I had the faith to see this battle through. I transported my mind back to this same scenario with Lauren, and I just couldn't believe this could happen to me yet again.

On the drive to the Children's Hospital, I remember praying, "God, if you aren't going to save my child, then just take her now. Please don't make me go through what I went through with Lauren. Please just heal her and let us go home. She will have an amazing testimony to tell the world. She still has so much life within her to give to You. Her story isn't done."

There are so many details of that day that seem to mesh together. Yet, I distinctly remember sitting in the family waiting room and looking into the general waiting room right next door. It is filled with Madison's friends who had come to pray and show their support for her. I remember thinking, my God, she has no idea how loved she really is. Madison viewed herself as a broken, unloved, fat girl who had no friends and wasn't good at anything. But the crowd in the waiting room told a different story. These young people would remain at the hospital for not just hours but days, only leaving to go to school or work. How could a child who thought so little of herself have so many people standing in unison and faith, believing the Lord would perform a miracle, and she would walk out of the hospital with a testimony to share with everyone? These beautiful humans loved my sweet girl, and I was genuinely grateful to know that at that very moment. It warmed my heart to see how much they all cared for her.

I often wonder how this single situation impacted their lives, faith, and destinies. I have remained in contact with a few of them. I watched as some walked away from God while others dashed towards Him. One thing that I have learned from Madison's life is that she lived in the moment. She loved without boundaries, gave of herself tirelessly, and shined God's love on all who crossed her path. She truly was a lighthouse for His glory to shine to the world. She simply lived a life that was pleasing in the eyes of the Lord. She didn't just tell people about God's love. She showed them His love through her actions. At just 17 years old, her life had impacted many. Her funeral was standing room only, with hundreds, possibly thousands more watching online.

Though broken, I was blessed. Blessed to say Madison was my child, my daughter, with whom I was well pleased.

A parent should never outlive their children, and while my heart and mind agree with this statement, my soul knows that the Lord knows best. Losing Lauren was debilitating. However, losing Madison was devastating. For almost half my life, I was known as Madison's mom. She was my purpose, my reason for living, and in a blink of an eye, my reason was gone. I struggled to find my place. I battled many dark moments and can remember lying on the couch and praying, "God, just let me fall asleep and not wake up." I didn't care if I woke up in Heaven or hell. I simply did not want to live here like this anymore. Not only was my heart crushed, but my spirit was crushed. God had taken everything from me. I would spend a year battling through those dark moments, trying desperately to figure it all out, knowing that I somehow needed to find my way back to the One who controlled it all. Remember, they were my lungs. I lived 17 years with one lung. Now I was supposed to be able to do so with none. How would that be possible? What I didn't know then was that impossibilities were His specialty. It is in the midst of impossibility that He makes all things possible. It was in the midst of this specific impossibility that I realized that He was my lungs. He was only lending me Lauren and Madison for a space of time in which to help me become who I am today. I know that sounds tragic. It doesn't sound loving. However, He has been there for me. In the darkest of nights, He has been there.

As the darkness and mourning began to subside, and I was starting to find joy again, tragedy would soon find its way back into my life. Clearly, I was a magnet for trauma. Just two years later, my husband of almost 15 years was told that the liver disease he thought he was managing had progressed so severely that he only had months to live. How could I be here again? What had I done that was so bad that God didn't want me to have anything or anyone to love or love me? There was no way that this would end the same way. Surely this would be the testimony I believed for with Lauren and Madison in the making. It had to be.

God had a purpose for my husband, which had not been fulfilled. Therefore, He wouldn't take him. Surely, He wouldn't. We still had to conquer the world together. There was still more work to do. I refused to accept this as the outcome. I began to fight the only way I knew how which was on my knees. I stood boldly on God's Word, professed healing, and denounced anyone who spoke differently. If you had no faith, you could not come anywhere near us. I knew this time, healing would come. How could it not? I was fighting harder than I had ever fought before. There was no way the devil would win this time. Reread part of what I was thinking here. I, not God, but I. What I failed to realize as I had with the losses of my daughters is that it was not about me. It was about them. God was doing what was best for them. I had to receive what His will for them was, whether I liked it or not. Who was I to think that what I wanted was better for them than what God wanted for them?

I hadn't died on a cross for any of them. Though I would have, I hadn't.

During the final months of his life, Sid found his way back to the Lord and made amends with many people. The Lord gave him the time he needed to secure his place in eternity. Though I was extremely grateful for that, I still could not believe I was facing such a monumental loss yet again. God had forsaken me yet again. I'm sorry, but that is what I was feeling. I had lost both of my twin girls, and now, I was losing my husband. How would I get up from this loss? This time I honestly did not know. I was oblivious to how I would stand again after Madison, but this, this was something totally different. How could He love me and yet take everything from me? I felt like a modern-day Job of sorts, yet I knew that my latter days would not be greater than the former. I would not be restored as Job was. I would simply exist until my last days. Christmas Eve, he passed away. God didn't heal him. God didn't show up in the way I believed Him to show up. If I thought I was crushed before, try disintegrated now.

This loss had obliterated my spirit. I believe it was the magnitude of all the losses put together that sent me reeling. The months after losing my husband became my own personal wilderness experience.

Everyone who had promised to be there seemed to disappear. All the tears, hugs, and fake sincerity that people gave me were just that, fake. Those who didn't disappear simply stayed away because they had no idea what to say or how to help. Maybe they felt as if I was a leper. Perhaps some thought that if they came around me, somehow this exact thing would happen to their family, and they couldn't take the chance of that happening to the people they loved the most. I was not worth the thought of a call, a text, a hug, or a lunch date. I was utterly alone. I had to deal with the deepest pain in my life by myself. While it didn't seem like it at the time, that wilderness experience was what I needed. It was during this time that I truly found the Lord. I began to know Him for myself and trust Him like never before. I knew that without Him, I could not make it. It was a long journey, but He carried me through. And as the darkness once again began to fade and mourning turned into dancing, I began to live again. Slowly but surely, I began to learn to breathe again. One breath at a time. Inhale. Exhale.

It was all I could do. I continued to trust His plan for my own life.

I continued to beckon Him to have His way in my life, and He continued to show up. He blessed me with another chance at life, love, and friends who fight with and for me. I can stand today and say that I am truly blessed beyond measure.

Though my life is filled with tragic moments, it's also filled with blessed moments. Valleys and mountaintops. Highs and lows. It's part of life. My life may seem harder than others, but there are also others whose lives seem harder than mine.

Even when I didn't feel like it and my actions didn't really portray it, I trusted God. God was there even when my heart was broken, and my spirit was absolutely crushed.

He was there to console, comfort, and hold me up when I felt there was no way I would ever be able to stand again. He sent others to gather around me and provide me with the support I needed.

The support I missed when I lost my late husband. The support in which I will need for a lifetime to come. He blessed me with friendships that I cherish. He has blessed me with a son I adore and the sweetest man ever created. He loves me through all my pain, loves me for me, and always has my back.

I could never replace all that I have lost. However, what I have gained sure enough makes my heart keep beating every day, my hands continue to raise in praise, and my feet keep taking steps toward the finish line.

Though I often wonder what life would be like if my girls and my husband were still here, those thoughts don't consume me like they once did. I have peace in knowing that each of them fought the good fight and earned their rewards. While I miss them with every fiber of my being, my story is not over. God is still writing it, and I am waiting in anticipation for all He has for me. I am still here, enduring until the end. I trust that His ways will always be greater than my own. That He fights battles that I never even know about. I know for a fact that no one could have pulled me out of the pit of despair I was drowning in but God. It was a task too tall for any human. It took a supernatural strength to get me to see the light again. So, if I can stay the course and continue the path after such significant losses, so can you.

You have the ability to keep fighting, to keep getting up every time you are knocked down. If you continue to include King Jesus in your plans, you will always win. It is when you let go of His steady hand that your path becomes crooked. If that is you today, if you have let go of Him, I urge you to find your way back to Him. I implore you to try again with Him at the head and center of it all.

You have the best chance when you are in lockstep with Him. You have the least chance when you want to continue walking to the beat of your own drum. It's okay to be down, it's okay to not be okay, but the important thing is that you never choose to stay there. The important thing is that you always let God help you get back up. God is still working some things out in my life, even now, to add even more richness to it. I'm at the edge of my seat, anticipating what He has in store. I could have given up when Lauren passed. I could have given up when Madison passed. I could have given up when Sid passed, even when my mom died. I didn't even mention that. She passed away just two years after Sid. Another loss, another dagger to the heart. Another justifiable reason to give up. The enemy probably expected me to. Many people probably expected me to, but not God. At my lowest points in life, in my weakest moments, He made me strong. If you take nothing else away from my chapter, lock this somewhere in a secret place, deep within your heart, and NEVER GIVE UP!

One day, I will be reunited with my girls for all eternity. Until that day, I have peace in knowing that they are where they belong. Until that day, I will share their stories and carry on their legacies so the world knows they were here. I will share our stories to let someone else know that God can and will use the least of us to reach the most of us. And for that, I will praise Him.

Fornication:

sexual intercourse between people not married to each other.

Soul ties are real. A soul tie is an inexplicable, powerful emotional bond to another person after being physically intimate with them. These are so serious that even when you try to sever the connection to that specific person you still feel as if they are connected to you. This brings on feelings of brokenness and leaves you feeling less than, as if you have lost a portion of yourself. Soul ties are a "side effect" of fornication. When you lay with someone, whom you are not married to, you run the risk of developing these soul ties and then you are left scrambling to figure out how to disconnect them.

Fornication is what connects these ties to the wrong people. The Bible says that man and wife become one (Mark 10:8), their souls become tied. When you chose to connect with someone in a sexual manner without being biblically married to them, you create a soul tie that was never meant to be formed. Daily, we wrestle not against flesh and blood but principalities and wickedness in high places (Ephesians 6:12). These ties begin to control our flesh and we have ungodly, fleshly appetites that we end up not being able to control.

Fornication can open the door to so many other vile spirits. We are commanded to treat our bodies as the temples God created them to be (1 Corinthians 6:19). That means that we should not defile them with immoral acts of sin. For when we choose to do so, we are subject to many other afflictions to come.

Fornication is driven by the spirit of lust. Lust is defined in the dictionary as a very strong sexual desire or an unbridled, intense sexual desire. It is also defined as an uncontrolled or illicit sexual appetite or a passionate overmastering desire or craving; lecherousness (unrestrained or excessive indulgence of sexual desire). Just typing these words makes me feel dirty, as if I should repent and take a shower. It sounds so sinful. Therefore, it can't be something that we should be involved in as Christians. We must not lust after the flesh (1 John 2:16) because it would have us portraying ourselves as if we are of this world and we are not. We are of the spirit, so we have to be mindful to always walk in the spirit and in truth (Galatians 5:16).

So, we must not only be mindful to guard ourselves from the lust of the flesh but we also must guard those around us as well. We have to be mindful of our language, our attire, the things we choose to entertain and the things we let into our homes. Doorways are opened sometimes unto others around us, especially our children, because we aren't guarding entrances like we should. Sometimes this happens out of ignorance. We ourselves are unaware of the dangers we place in their paths by allowing things that seem innocent but include little nuances that insinuate lustful or sinful desires without us even picking up on it. If you don't believe me, check out some of the cartoons, movies and tv shows that some of these "kiddie channels" are putting out now. It's all an open door that will lead them on a path of fornication later in life, possibly sooner, because they are introduced to the idea at such young ages when their minds are being trained on what to accept as "normal" and what to believe.

For girls, it is gravely important that they have their fathers in their lives. Young girls have a need for validation, love and support. When those elements are missing from their adolescent years, they are more vulnerable to the spirit of lust or fornication because they are searching to fill a void, they do not even understand why they have.

There are also other situations where we are just inquisitive and want to "try our luck" to see what's out there. Especially for a young person who has grown up in church but has witnessed so many of their peers live a different life than them. Those peers seem to get to have all the fun, while they feel restricted to a different lifestyle. There should be conversations discussed, around these topics to help them understand the dangers that can and will arise. We shouldn't just be saying "don't do this" or "don't do that", but we should be offering an explanation as to why we don't do this or that and though it is good enough, it shouldn't just be "because the Bible says." Unfortunately, some people need more than just that. They shouldn't, but they do.

When a child is young and we are in the kitchen preparing dinner while allowing them to wonder around aimlessly on the floor and they get close to the stove we say "Aht, don't touch that, because it's hot and it will burn you." We offer them the reason behind our instruction. The same should be for so many other topics that they will have to deal with in their lives, one of them being the importance of celibacy and not dabbling in fornication.

You are a treasure to God (1 Peter 2:9). You are worth more than a quick fix or a one-night stand. Make the choice not to allow your body to be overtaken by fleshly thoughts and desires but to daily strive to make it a temple holy and acceptable unto God. You will not only be doing what is right according to God's word but you will be doing what's right for yourself and those who watch your walk with God, whether you know their eyes or on you or not.

Choose the Spirit instead of the flesh and ask the Lord to help you make that choice each and every day. It will provide you with mental clarity and godly pride that you are able to deny the enemy and your flesh and honor the Lord with your mind, body, and spirit.

1 Corinthians 6:18-20 AMP Run away from sexual immorality (in any form, whether thought or behavior, whether visual or written). Every other sin that a man commits is outside the body, but the one who is sexually immoral sins against his own body. Do you not know that your body is a temple of the Holy Spirit who is within you, whom you have (received as a gift, from God, and that you are not your own property? You were bought with a price (you were actually purchased with the precious blood of Jesus and made His own). So then, honor and glorify God with your body.

1 John 2:15-16 AMP Do not love the world (of sin that opposes God and His precepts), nor the things that are in the world. If anyone loves the world, the love of the Father is not in him. For all that is in the world – the lust and sensual craving of the flesh and the lust and longing of the eyes and the boastful pride of life (pretentious confidence in one's resources or in the stability of earthly things) – these do not come from the Father, but are from the world.

Galatians 5:16-17 AMP But I say, walk habitually in the Holy Spirit (seek Him and be responsive to His guidance), and then you will certainly not carry out the desire of the sinful nature (which responds impulsively without regard for God and His precepts). For the sinful nature has its desire which is opposed to the Spirit, and the (desire of the) Spirit opposes the sinful nature; for these two, (the sinful nature and the Spirit) are in direct opposition to each other (continually in conflict), so that you (as believers) do not (always) do whatever (good things) you want to do.

Revelations 21:8 AMP But as for the cowards and unbelieving and abominable (who are devoid of character and personal integrity and practice or tolerate immorality), and murderers, and sorcerers (with intoxicating drugs), and idolaters and occultists (who practice and teach false religions), and all the liars (who knowingly deceive and twist truth), their part will be in the lake that blazes with fire and brimstone, which is the second death.

Colossians 3:5 AMP So put to death and deprive of power the evil longings of your earthly body (with its sensual, self-centered instincts) immorality, impurity, sinful passion, evil desire, and greed, which is (a kind of) idolatry (because it replaces your devotion to God).

Catrisha Shawnette Wilson is a hard-working, dedicated, prayerful woman of God. The gospel of Jesus Christ is her first love. She is a 42-year-old mother of 3, Serenity, Kaleb & Madison, who resides in New Albany, IN, though she was born and raised right across the bridge in Louisville, KY. Currently, she is employed with Humana in their Human Resources department.

She is actively involved at her church, HOPE Ministries, located in the west end of Louisville, where she has been a member for 16 years. She serves on several ministries at her church because she is willing to give whatever she can to keep as many souls out of hell as possible.

Catrisha loves serving others, praying with and for others and listening to gospel music while she enjoys relaxing at home. Her favorite worship song right now is God Provides because it speaks to her heart. The altar is her favorite place to be, communing with God and interceding for others.

She is big on family; her family is very important to her. She is very close with her parents, grandparents, siblings, in-laws, nieces, nephews, and cousins. Family is a top priority in her life.

When asked about including a chapter in this book, Catrisha immediately felt a nudge of the Holy Ghost to be a part of it. She decided she wouldn't shy away from giving her testimony in hopes of allowing someone else, who may be stuck in the same type of situations she was, to know that they aren't alone and that they can come out of it. She wanted to be as transparent as possible so that the glory of God could show through the words on every page in hopes of touching the heart connected to the hands turning those same pages.

Catrisha's life is proof that God can and will use you if you let Him. Her life is evidence of God's DNA and His power. You can often hear her quoted saying, "Just stand" or "I'm still standing" because she believes God will do the rest if she just decides to stand. Her prayer is that her words touch the lives of a 16-year-old girl or 40-year-old woman or a 20-year-old single mom who is at the end of the rope, barely hanging on. She wants them to know that Jesus is worth the try. If you make the choice to give Him a try, you won't regret it. He truly is all that we all will ever need. **Proverbs 31:25 KJV Strength and honour are her clothing; And she shall rejoice in time to come.**

Still Standing

As my mind begins to roll back to my early childhood years, I remember that I was always curious about what it felt like to be in an intimate relationship. I don't even really understand why I had those feelings then, but I did. I don't know where they began to come from, however at a young age I would sit and daydream about what it felt like to be loved or touched, period. These thoughts were always very foreign to me. I couldn't seem to get rid of them, no matter how hard I tried. They would come to my mind often. I know that most people, or at least I hear, that some women who have these promiscuous tendencies have some sort of trauma attached to it. They grow up in single parent homes, with the mom being the only parent, without a father. They are inappropriately touched at an early age. They are introduced to things they shouldn't be at an early age. None of these situations had been the case for me. I grew up in a two-parent home and I was never touched inappropriately or had any interactions that would spark such a curiosity within me, but for some reason I had this curiosity about love; what it actually was and how it actually felt.

Even then, I remember sitting days in and out praying and asking God for the things I wanted and needed, or so I thought. I didn't even understand what I was saying or who I was speaking to in that moment. However, there was something inside of me that felt like I needed to feel something or experience something. I didn't even know what that something looked like or felt like, I just knew that it was something that I wanted to touch or be touched by. Even in my adult years now, I think back and wonder, what intrigued me to even begin having those thoughts, feelings, wants and desires then. Of course, now that I am older and I have grown in my walk with God, I do realize that it was a spirit. Spirits are real and they will attach themselves to you if you are not careful. If we open the door, please believe a spirit will walk through it. I can see now that the enemy was after me at a very young age. Please believe he is on assignment just as much as we are. It was him who planted those thoughts, feelings and desires within me because he knew that he would try to use those same seeds to allow a tree so big to sprout within me that I wouldn't be able to cut it down. Keep reading, because believe you me, I became a lumberjack

September 2020 and I wouldn't trade that decision for the world!

So, after turning 16 and deciding that I was woman enough, I mean come on, the nerve of me right. Ha! It's funny now looking back in my 40's to the younger version of myself and thinking about some of the decisions I made. How foolish I was in my youth to believe that I was strong enough to handle such a thing. But God. Again, I decide I am woman enough to start my journey of fornication. I had my first encounter with being with someone who I just knew was my everything. Not God, who is spotless and blameless, but a man in which such a great God created who had flesh just like me. I thought that he could be my everything because I was oblivious to the fact then, that only God could be that for me. I would learn, the hard way of course. Because this person was not only so far from my everything but they took me down a deep, dark hole that started a lengthy line of desires, wants and needs that I would continue to crave for years to come. We look at addicts as being those who are addicted to drugs and alcohol only. No ma'am, no sir. I craved skin-to-skin contact as if I couldn't live without it. I was literally craving to get a "fix" constantly and I couldn't even suppress it. I had no control over it. I was searching for the taste of what I thought was love. I didn't even understand, couldn't even comprehend at the young age of 16 the true depths of what love was between two people. All I knew was ok, here is this guy that I feel like I love and I believed that he loved me and I assumed that what we did together produced love. This was my first encounter with the spirit of fornication. If I knew then what I know now, would I make a different choice? Absolutely! Of course, I would make a better choice because that one decision caused me years of pain, heartbreak and disappointment. If I can be honest, it still sometimes pains me when I think about being a single mother to 3 of the most amazing kids a person could meet. It pains me when I think about the fact that I am 42 and still unmarried. It pains me because the enemy still uses it as a tactic to make me believe that I am unworthy of true love. However, it has also strengthened me to stay the course. It has also given me a power that I didn't possess at 16 to fight the enemy and make him the liar that he is. I serve a great big God who can do all things, except fail. He hasn't failed me up until now and He won't fail me in the future. He is my everything now. He is the love of my life and I trust His plan for it. I wish I would have traded my will for His long ago, but I didn't. But now that I have, my life has changed for the better.

So, at 16 I just knew that this would be the love of my life. This is what happiness is going to look like. This is what joy is going to look like. At 16! I could barely apply for a job but here I thought I could be someone's wife and raise a family and be good for life. It's preposterous how we think sometimes y'all. I can laugh now, though it really isn't funny, it tickles me to think of how naïve I really was then. You could not tell me that this wasn't what it meant to be loved by another human being. Quickly at the same age I realized I had made a mistake. I found myself in this dark hole that I had no idea how to get out of. So, what do I do now? How do you get out when you don't know the way? You don't. You dig deeper and deeper into the pit because obviously this is where you belong. So, after that encounter I found myself introducing myself to multiple partners for many years to come. My body began to have an insatiable desire for fornication. Unfortunately for me, I ended up making some choices that left me with the inevitable doctor's visits that I could have avoided. It also introduced me to other worldly desires such as drinking. You see because this is the thing, once we open one door, it gives way for many others to be opened as well. My spirit was not being guarded and so, it was open season on my salvation. The enemy would use whatever he could to keep me from becoming who he knew God had destined me to be from the womb. The enemy introduced me to alcohol to cover up the sin of fornication. Alcohol was the solution for the self-inflicted pain I was daily finding myself in. I would dabble with drinking to cover up the sorrow I felt deep within my soul. Let me tell y'all now, it never worked. It never did anything to soothe the gaping hole I had created because the only place filler for that hole was Jesus. Every time I released myself to another human being, I fell deeper in the hole. It all started at that tender age of 16. I wonder sometimes what 16 even means. It was then that I decided to walk through this door that was before me. This door that I walked through also opened other doors, as I explained above, and I was feeling things I had never felt before. I felt hatred, bitterness, sorrow and depression, constantly. I was daily living with all of these aches and pains that I was never meant to experience. I began having crying spells and deep feelings within me that were causing me deep turmoil. It was like a spiritual war within me of twisting and turning because at the age of 16 I decided to open the door to fornication. I know that in our youth we don't even fully understand that the decisions we make then will set the tone for the rest of our lives. We have to live with those decisions forever. However, we don't have to stay in those places. We don't have to be labeled those things God brought us out of. We can make better choices and become new creatures through Him. I am so thankful for grace and mercy on today because it is what has kept me. I am so thankful for His blood and His name because it is what saved me.

That person that I decided to go on a journey with at the age of 16 eventually decided that he would go on about his business and that business would no longer include me. After he had delivered the packages of fornication, pain, brokenness, drinking and sorrow he decided to go his own separate way, without me. It left me in a pit of despair. I had to figure out how I would get released from this place, this dungeon of sorts that I had created for myself. I looked up and I was 20. I began to look back and I realized I had done so many things in those short years between 16 and 20 that I never thought I would do and so now I was also dealing with the feelings of shame and condemnation. How in the world would I get up from here? Would I find Jesus now, would I turn to Him then in this state of brokenness? Nope, unfortunately, not yet. I then meet an older gentleman, or so I thought. One who is much different from my 16-year-old introduction to pain and misery. This one was different. Surely this was the love and joy I thought I had found at 16. This one REALLY loved me. Or did he? Honey, no. This one wasn't the prize I was looking for either. I should have left that joker in the bottom of the cracker jack box he wanted to be content in. This one showed me how not to respect myself, how not to love myself and how not to care for myself. Now, here I am at 20, traveling another road, taking another journey but still going the wrong way. The hole I thought could get no deeper, did. I had more doctor's visits, more pills and oh, now my spirit had been opened to pornography. An individual already struggling to suppress desires and ungodly thoughts when it came to intimacy now was introduced to the holy grail of said things. As if that wasn't enough, I was now also smoking. The things I found myself engaging in were not me. I was never that person. I knew this! However, here I was showing up as that person every single day. Faking it until you make it can sometimes be a dangerous game of Russian roulette. Even though I wanted to, I couldn't say no. I didn't know how. So, I continued to pretend to be who I thought he wanted me to be all in the name of love. Well, now I can say in the name of lust because it never was love. I continued to sit and fester in that dark hole. Fast-forward to the age 25 and now I have birthed a child with this individual. Fast-forward again and I have birthed a second child. Fast-forward one more time and I have birthed a third child with him. Now I am 30. My youth is over. I am a mother of 3 amazing babies but I have been left by "the love of my life" to raise them alone. This was never how I dreamed of my life. This was not the fairytale ending, the white picket fence, the perfectly manicured lawn I had saw in my dreams all those years ago.

One day, at the age of 30, I can just remember deciding that my life had to change. I could no longer keep living that way. I remember my mother praying, crying, begging and pleading for me to live right. I remember her standing on the word of God, fasting and believing God was going to turn it around. She didn't even completely understand what exactly was going on with her eldest child, but she knew that she couldn't stand by and just let life happen to me. She knew that it was detrimental to my livelihood that she stood in the gap for my soul at a time when I could not stand for myself. She kept doing what she knew to do to touch heaven. She kept living as an obedient example before me so that I could have a blueprint of how to live for God. Through all the hurt, pain, trials, and life-changing circumstances in my early years, I remember one day, God came and He met me right where I was. I remember this still soft voice speaking to me. Caressing and mending my heart with the whispers from His lips. I remember feeling peace in His presence and a joy I never experienced before in the moments that He spoke to me.

If you get nothing else out of reading this chapter, please understand this, there is a God that loves you and will come to your rescue. Sometimes we don't even realize we need to be rescued. Sometimes we don't think we can be rescued. We feel as if we have gone too far or done too much, but God. God is sovereign, just and gracious to forgive us. He is also jealous and vengeful, so please don't mistake his grace, mercy or kindness for weakness. It is His never-ending love that keeps us. He will embrace you. He will come and show you exactly what true love is. Not what we think, but the real thing. Not what our flesh tends to try to create as real love, not that mirage, but the real thing. He provides us with tangible, life-altering, agape love! God knows the type of love we need. He is a gentleman, so He just patiently waits until we realize that, that type of love, begins with Him. I am standing here today, living a holy, righteous life, fighting, each and every day because of His love. I am determined to keep on walking. I am determined to keep on pushing. I am determined to keep on praying. I am determined to keep on running! For the race is not given to the swift, but to those who endure until the end. I am enduring! I am determined to keep my torch lifted high while running this race and telling my story to help others along their paths, but to also help myself gain strength daily. To be able to look back and see where God carried me, to see that one set of footprints in my story, to see the transition from victim to victor, is a beautiful thing. I made myself a victim, at the young age of 16, that's when it began. However, God never meant for me to become that. He always meant for me to be a victor and that's what I am today. I have the victory over promiscuity, fornication, bitterness, hatred and rebellion. I am no longer what the enemy tried to make me believe I was, all those years ago. Today, I stand godly-proud of who God has allowed me to become. I'm no longer living a life of fornication. I am standing strong, filled with hope and the faith that I can make it and I can be who God has always destined me to be. I do not need fornication, lust or love from the wrong places to define who I am. God does that for me. He defines me. I have all that I need because I have Jesus. There is nothing more in this life that I need outside of Him. Once you understand that you have Him and you allow Him to lead you and map out your destiny, you will come to the realization that it is absolutely worth it. It is worth every trial, tribulation, wound and pit you dug for yourself, to follow Him. He is our savior. The only savior we have.

If you don't know Him, please get to know Him. Please find someone that you can trust that will help you get to know Him like I know Him. Find someone who doesn't mind teaching you about His commandments, about His love, about His power. Open the Bible and study for yourself, who He is. Begin your relationship with Him right now, if you don't have one. If you have walked away from your relationship with Him, return to it. You won't find a better life outside of Him. His will is the safest place for any of us to be. Fall on your knees and ask for forgiveness. Lift your hands and surrender to Him your will in exchange for His. It will be the best decision you will ever make. Understand this, when you feel as if you cannot take another step, as if life has the upper hand and you are completely drained of strength to keep going, know that He is there. Even when it seems like He isn't or He is far away, He is there. He is watching out for you, covering you and collecting your tears. He is preparing a way for you, even when there seems to be no way in sight. He is the God of clear paths. He clears paths for each of us, in order for us to become who He created us to be in the first place. When you find yourself in those places, pick up the Word, get in a prayer closet, push back the plate and seek Him. He will meet you right where you are. He will provide shelter from storms and the navigation needed to make it through. He is our

GPS. As long as we decide to stay on His radar, there's no way we can get lost.

It is in all of our best interests to live a righteous, holy life. A life set apart from evil and sin. A life set a part from this world. We can live a clean and beautiful life in Him. When you make up your mind and you decide that you are tired of being tired is when God will show up, because He is our strength in our weaknesses. That is the moment that He will step in and say, thank you, this is right where I needed you. Now that you have laid down what you thought was best for your life, I can give you the plans I have held in my hand all this time. For I know the plans that I have for you, plans to prosper you and give you an expected end, Jeremiah 29:11. That's what happened to me. I laid down fornication. I laid down lust. I laid down my will. I laid down my life, in exchange for His. My life, hasn't been and never will be the same, because I chose Him.

The year is 2020 and God has blessed me to come all these years from the age of 16 and I am now 40. I remember the smell of sanitation and machinery. I remember the sound of the beeping machines nursing my anxiety and causing me to second guess everything I've ever made the wrong decision about in my life. I remember thinking of my kids and wondering if things were going to get worse or get better. I wondered if I would be able to get home to them again and watch them graduate high school, get married and have children of their own. I had pneumonia in both lungs and I had been diagnosed with COVID. I had heard all of the horror stories of people young and old succumbing to this disease and I refused to become one of the enemy's statistics. I was determined to get better and to live a healthier and holier life like never before, as soon as I could get out of there. I was told that I didn't have any fight in me and I wasn't progressing in the manner in which the doctor's wanted me to. They had decided that it was in my best medical interest to be placed on a ventilator. I had heard over and over, not to let that happen. So many people passed away once they had been placed on the ventilator and I had no intentions of allowing that to be my story. They even told me that if I went on the ventilator that there was a serious possibility that I would pass away. Who in their right mind would accept such fate from someone who was not God? I may not have been perfect or living holy as I should have been at the time, but I did know the power of prayer. I did have great faith and I trusted and believed that God had greater plans for me than letting me succumb to my situation at that time. If He could keep His hand on my life all of those years before, surely 2020 was no match for a God so great! This all happened to me in the summer of 2020. At 40 years old, I was walking around dragging an oxygen tank behind me. I was struggling to get from my bed to the bathroom without taking a break for my lungs to catch up with my movements. But guess what, I was breathing. I was here. I was alive! I remember going to night service and going to the altar because I was tired of dragging this oxygen tank around behind me like it was really some sort of adorned accessory. I decided earlier that day at afternoon service that I was no longer accepting that. I was about to stand on my faith and let God do what His word says He would, take care of me. Jehovah Rapha showed Himself mighty that night. I laid that tank down, allowed the strap to slip from my shoulder and went to shouting and praising God. It was so hard for me to breathe but I believed God, so if I was going out, then I was going out praising but I knew His word to be true. If He had healed me before, surely, He could heal me again. He did just that. I returned that tank back from whence it came the very next day. He filled my lungs with His breath every day from that day forth and I am alive today because of Him!

Fast-forward, it is now September 2020. I had my last encounter with fooling around with sin. I had made up my mind that I could no longer keep playing in sin's playground. I could no longer continue down the path I started some almost 25 years ago. I had finally had enough of allowing sin to suffocate me and hold me captive in a prison that I had the key to. I decided that I was going to move forward and give it all up so that I could allow God to do what He wanted to do in my life. I can't believe it took me that long to do that, but it did. It was the best decision I've made in all my life, genuinely giving my life to Christ. The death of my flesh was the birth of my life. It was the beginning of me actually starting to live the way God wanted me to all those years ago. I had one heck of a detour, but I believe like never before that I am headed toward the right destination now. I stood ten toes down, looked sin in the face and said never again. I will not go down that path or dabble in rebuilding that mess of a tower again. God had brought me through a mighty test and the least I could do is repay Him with my life. I could never truly repay Him, but I could try my best to give Him everything I have to offer. God has kept me, loved me, protected me and guided me. Why would I give in now? I am not going to give in. All those prayers prayed with my own lips and the lips of others on my behalf were not in vain. They would come to fruition because the prayers of the righteous truly do avail much! All the tears, all the loneliness, all the times I felt so weary and downtrodden, thinking I wasn't going to make it, fueled me to endure. All the times I decided to abandon God, He chose to never abandon me. He was always there. This is why I can't turn my back on Him ever again. I can't "slap Him in the face" with my actions after all He has done and continues to do for me and my children.

I recall sitting in my bedroom hearing "you're going to die". It stopped me in my tracks and made me really take a moment to think and to be honest with myself. What in the world was going on? It wasn't just the words but the way in which I heard them. "You're going to die." There it was again, a still, small voice. It was as if it was whispering to me and that made it that much more bone chilling. I turned to the guy beside me and told him I could no longer do this and he needed to leave. He got up and he left. I woke up my children when he was gone and I had them all come stay in my room with me. At least I would get one last day with them by my side. I'm sure they were so confused and worried. They had just experienced such trauma with my hospital stay just months before. I chose life that day. That was the day I chose to live not just for myself or my children but finally for God. I chose to live the life God had chosen for me at 16, finally at 40. I decided that I was going to begin right then and there to really begin to follow Christ. I refused to go to a burning hell over a touch or a few moments of pleasure. It is not worth it at 40 and it definitely wasn't worth it at 16. I wish I would have realized that long before then. I was not about to allow temptations, thoughts or feelings to overtake me. It was in that moment that I understood God's true love for me. It wasn't easy. Please believe me. It was probably, easily one of the hardest things I've ever done. That didn't stop me from taking another step each and every day towards God's plan for my life. It is in those tough moments that you have to get close to those who will pray for you. People who will intercede for you. People who will be genuine in supporting you on your walk with God. You can't be around spiritually anemic people in those moments. You have to be around people of power who will charge hell for your soul. The truth is that sometimes we are in seasons that we aren't strong enough to handle things on our own. In those seasons, we have to have warriors who don't mind slaying giants for us. People that will tell you right from wrong, whether we already know it or not. We have to have accountability partners that don't mind correcting our missteps in order to get us back on the right path. People we trust with our lives and allow to encourage us to live holy. We need people who will not take what we tell them and share it with the world. Those type of people who will not gossip about our troubles but will take our worries to the throne of God on our behalf in hopes of us being set free from chains that hold us back from our destinies. You need people of strength that will help you come out of bad situations and help you to grow. We must have people in our corners that will help in the edification of our spirits. I had an amazing prayerful support system, beginning long time ago with my mother and grandmother. I had sisters and brothers in Christ, both in the natural and the spirit. Prayers of one of the sister's that is creating this book right now. My sister Gina. Blood couldn't make us any more family than we already are. She checked on me daily, she never talked about me, she let me bare my soul to her whenever I needed to and intently listened to the words I spoke. She would let me get out whatever was on my heart but she would also give me sound Biblical advice about whatever we were discussing. She would give me the big girl pep talk. She would say things to me like, "it's time to get up, you have to fight, you have to get back to that place where you know what to do". She would not allow me to wallow in the mud with pigs because she knew my Father was waiting to welcome me home. She would not allow me to be comfortable in my sin. She wouldn't broadcast it, but she wouldn't accept it either. She wouldn't just say aww girl, it will be ok, all of us fall. No, she would respond with the word and prayer. She would remind me who I was. She would not allow me to remain depressed or in the state of mind I had found myself in. She would fight, alongside with me. It was her friendship that helped uphold me. All glory belongs to God, but He definitely uses people in our lives to dig us out of pits. As I told you all early on in this chapter, I had dug quite a pit for myself. I am so glad that I had people that were not afraid of grabbing spiritual shovels and removing all the excess mess I had created. However, it is my sister who had a huge part in you all being able to read these words on the pages of this book today. It was her push for me to stand up to the enemy and take my life back that allowed me to share this testimony of God's goodness with the world, in hopes of someone who may be struggling in the way in which I was to know that God can and will help them out of it, if they chose to let Him. If you decide to stand up to the enemy right now and take back your life, God will equip you with supernatural strength to handle everything the enemy will try to block your path. I truly hope that my story blesses everyone who reads it, whether they have had a similar experience or not. If God loved you in abundance while living in sin, how much more could He love you in His will? My God, just thinking of His love sends chills through me. I am eternally grateful for His grace and mercy that covered and continues to cover me. I am able to be a true example to my own children now because of this new chance at life given to me by God. Once you are serving God, you will find so many treasures along the journey. It is a fight, but it's a fight that is worth your life.

It is a fight that is worth fighting. Not just for your sake but for the sake of others who are watching you, because believe me, people are watching you. People in your family, in your community and on your job. Your fight is fuel to the fight of others. So, chose to fight! You can do this! No matter what anyone else may say, just take one day at a time. You can do this! We all can do all things through Christ. He truly does strengthen us. Take one step at a time. Do not give up. Please believe, I was at a starting point before also. I was stressed, weary, sin riddled and broken. But not anymore. I am restored, blessed, healthy, happy and made whole by the God of the universe. I continued to fight. I won't stop fighting. I will continue to press and push towards the mark of the higher calling set forth for my life. I pray that this chapter truly blesses someone and causes you to turn your life over to Christ. You will never regret that decision. It will always be the best decision that you ever make. I am a ProdiGAL!

Suicide:

The act or an instance of taking one's own life voluntarily and intentionally. Being or performing a deliberate act resulting in the voluntary death of the person who does it.

I'm sure we all think of suicide and we automatically think, not us. However, you would be surprised how many people in the same room with you have contemplated and sadly, even attempted suicide. After reading some statistics on the internet, I gathered the following. Suicide is the second leading cause of death (after accidents) for people aged 10 to 34. This is a serious health crisis, even more so, a spiritual crisis. The year 2020 was a tumultuous year for the world. There were 45,979 noted Americans who died by suicide. On average, there are 130 suicides per day. There were an estimated 1.2 million failed suicide attempts. Praise God for that!

Men were said to have died by suicide 3.88 times more than women. This speaks to me so loudly because I look at it as a tactic of the enemy. Suicide is a weapon he has etched in his tool belt to try to stop the plan of God for so many people's lives. Gods order is designed for men to lead. If men are killing themselves at a higher rate than women, then that leaves more room for the world to be in chaos and out of order. So, the enemy uses this vicious tactic to take out leaders so that those who are supposed to be covered by them are left without the covering they need. It is definitely an assault on the structure in which God set in place for the family unit. This gives us great cause to pray. We must pray against the travesty of suicide because it causes the one committing the act to believe that it is their only option and that's absolutely false. God will always offer us a means of escape (1 Corinthians 10:13).

Most articles link suicide to mental disorders. Mental health is so important and vital to having a healthy, thriving life. We have to learn to take care of our mental health just as much as we do our physical bodies and our spiritual walks. I think that sometimes we don't want to deal with mental health issues because we don't want to be looked at as crazy or weak, more the latter than the former. We are too busy upholding an image we have portrayed for so long to take the necessary precautions to ensure that we are mentally well. This is a problem.

So many of us have been strong for so long, that we can't let others see our humanness. Vulnerability is equated with weakness in our minds and so we refuse to seek the help we need when we are struggling with our thoughts. The Bible says that the Lord will give us a shepherd (Jeremiah 3:15). I believe that we should always be able to confide in our leadership. I know that other people feel as if pastors do not have the authority to deal with mental health if they haven't gone to school for it or trained in the educational systems of the world, but I disagree. True men of God, are called by God. Therefore, they are God's mouthpiece and God can download what they need to say to you in an instant and it can give you the hope, peace and strength you are looking for in that moment to keep pressing forward.

I am not saying not to seek professional help from licensed counselors, to each their own, but what I am saying is that you should have a relationship with your spiritual leaders where you feel comfortable enough to have these hard conversations with them and feel like you can trust them to remain in the confines of the space you discuss your vulnerabilities with them in. You should be able to trust that what they speak into your life is only to edify you and help you be the best version of yourself. If you don't have this, you may want to reevaluate that situation.

Find somebody to talk to. Not just anyone, but someone you can trust. I believe this is part of the reason people choose to speak to therapists also. So many of our experiences in life teach us not to trust people so we don't want to open up and let our secrets out to people who know us from fear of being judged or it being brought up in a future conversation that will cause harm to our hearts. People can be ruthless and sometimes when people are angry, they forget to sin not. So, people go to therapists to get advice and to just let out feelings they don't feel they can safely express in the spaces that they are in.

I believe communication is so detrimental because it is therapeutic in nature. Effective communication is the basis of all relationships in our lives. So, if we are holding things in and refusing to let them out and release them, then we will become overwhelmed with those things. Then, once we are overwhelmed, all of those emotions have to make an escape in some way and I think this is how we get to a suicidal mindset. We allow our thoughts to run rampant and everything seems so out of control that we give up trying to correct any of it. Suicide seems to be the easiest answer for mounting debt, troubled children, failed marriages and disappointment after disappointment. If we are no longer here, then we no longer have to bear the burden or feel the weight, pressure, pain or grief of all that we are enduring in that specific season and all the seasons before or any of the seasons to come.

Exodus 20:13 AMP You shall not commit murder (unjustified, deliberate homicide).

1 Corinthians 10:13 AMP No temptation (regardless of its source) has overtaken or enticed you that is not common to human experience (nor is any temptation unusual or beyond human resistance); but God is faithful (to His word – He is compassionate and trustworthy), and He will not let you be tempted beyond your ability (to resist), but along with the temptation He (has in the past and is now and) will (always) provide the way out as well, so that you will be able to endure it (without yielding, and will overcome temptation with joy).

James 1:2-4 AMP Consider it nothing but joy, my brothers and sisters, whenever you fall into various trials. Be assured that the testing of your faith (through experience) produces endurance (leading to spiritual maturity, and inner peace). And let endurance have its perfect result and do a thorough work, so that you may be perfect and completely developed (in your faith), lacking nothing.

1 John 1:9 AMP If we (freely) admit that we have sinned and confess our sins, He is faithful and just (true to His own nature and promises), and will forgive our sins and cleans us continually from all unrighteousness (our wrongdoing, everything not in conformity with His will and purpose).

Romans 6:23 AMP For the wages of sin is death, but the free gift of God (that is, His remarkable, overwhelming gift of grace to believers) is eternal life in Christ Jesus our Lord.

Courtney Chenee' Parker is a 33-year-old woman who is wife to Vandrick Parker and mother of Amaria Parker. She resides in Louisville, KY where she has been all of her life. Courtney is the proud owner of Candidly Court, a blog that is based off of Faith, Family, and Friends. She uses her experiences in life and her faith to encourage others to see that no matter where you are in life, God can and will change things for you if you believe, trust, and allow Him to have complete control over your life.

Courtney is a millennial who is absolutely on fire for God. She is willing to share her testimony with anyone that will listen. She is the oldest of three siblings and the second oldest of fourteen grandchildren. In her spare time, Courtney loves to read, write, craft (Corkie's Wreaths and things) sing, dance, decorate, and help others.

Often known for wearing her heart on her sleeve, Courtney's heart beats to help others and she will do that anytime and at any place. Known as the blunt, comical one of the bunch, she takes her faith seriously and you can oftentimes find her praying over things and people's situations faithfully. She is currently a teacher's assistant at JCPS and prayerfully hopes to start school again August 2022 to accomplish her life-long dream of becoming a preschool teacher.

Courtney is no stranger to Christ and faith. Growing up as a PK (preacher's kid) introduced her to the idea of God, but it wasn't until she was up against things, she couldn't control that she started to take on the fullness of who God was and take Him at His word. It was then that she began to believe exactly what He says about her. Her favorite verse is Romans 8:18 **"For I consider that the sufferings of this present time are not worth comparing with the glory that is going to be revealed to us."** Courtney uses her test as a testimony and her mess as a message in order to assist other women that may or may not be in the same situations she once was. She uses her experiences to help others see that they too can break free of what the enemy says they are and walk in their God-given purpose!

Hello! My Name is Overcomer

"You're not enough."

"You will never be enough."

"The world would be a better place without you."

"Nobody will believe that you didn't ask for it."

"You must've made God mad otherwise why would you be losing so many family members back-to-back."

"Am I cursed?"

"I feel like death is following me and since it can't attack me, it's taking my family members away instead."

Many times, than I care to admit, I would believe the lies that the enemy was feeding to me, although, I knew differently. I knew that He felt threatened by me and the calling I had on my life, but I still chose to listen to the voices inside my head that were nothing but lies. I still believed the vomit that he was trying to make me return to daily.

My story is a typical one, but I feel an impactful one. I am a daughter of a preacher and granddaughter of a deacon, so I am really familiar with the house of God. Church was my second home, naturally. However, I never really thought much about it because I just figured it was what I was supposed to do. My relationship with God was on autopilot in my early years of life. I just did what I thought was expected of me. Routine attendance was all I knew at the time. I got baptized at the age of six and although I was serious about my walk, I got off track. Experiencing rape and molestation at such an early age will have that effect on you. Although that particular part of my story wasn't pretty and I would have never chosen for that to be a part of my testimony, I'm grateful that I am able to use that experience to tell my story in order to inspire and encourage others. Knowing how far I have come since those experiences is a vivid reminder of my growth when it seems as if I'm not making any progress. That sounds weird to most, being grateful for being raped and sexually molested but for me, it changed the trajectory of my life and made me into the person I am today. So, while I'm not celebrating the evil acts that I had to endure, I am celebrating the strength of a God so great that He would keep me from unbelief, bitterness, and hatred. I realize that going through those experiences and everything else that I've had to endure so far, has equipped me to help others get through their own trials and tribulations as well. If I had to go through to get to, I'm okay with that. I am okay with the God of the universe using me as a vessel, as a conduit, in which His power can flow to reach another soul.

Shortly after that ungodly ordeal, I started doubting God and thinking that He didn't love me. Though I couldn't see it then, I can see it now that those thoughts were being planted in my mind by the enemy to keep me from seeing who I really was in God. I know now that those thoughts were simply a trick from the enemy not wanting me to reach my potential and be the best version of myself. It caused me to doubt myself and doubt God. How could I doubt a blameless God? However, I began to think that God wasn't faithful to me so why should I be faithful to Him? He clearly doesn't want the best for me nor love me like He claims He does in that leatherbound book I heard people preach from all my life. Let me say this, let me make something clear right here. If I didn't learn anything from that situation, there is one thing I did gather from it. We have to know who we are in God and that will help us sift through the mess that the enemy tries to kill us with. One thing I will say is this, the devil is a hater, liar, and a manipulator. I used to be a ball of anger. I was angry with God, with life, with my abusers and with myself for believing the lies. I was angry that I, even for a second (years really), believed that I deserved what happened to me and that I would never be whole again. God made it fail though. He would eventually restore me.

A broken, bruised, bloody mess inside, I still attended church. I still showed up every service marking off my attendance box, saying "here" when I was so far from a relationship with God, sitting on a pew in His house. I kept showing up because it was part of my requirement. So, I kept going through the motions. I showed up and participated in various ministries, including singing in the choir and dance ministry. I was there physically, but mentally and spiritually, I was lightyears away from the services and my relationship with God. I wasn't getting anything out of it because I had allowed my heart to be hardened by circumstance. I didn't have any desire to let God in because it was His fault. He was the one that allowed the rape and molestation to happen in the first place.

I opted for the straightforward way out, suicide. If I were no longer here, I wouldn't have to suffer from the hollowness within me. I wouldn't have to pretend to be someone I didn't feel like. I didn't have to face the fact that I was damaged goods, and nobody buys the dented cans on the shelf. They usually end up discarded in a discount pile or simply thrown anyway. Why would I want to stay here in these conditions? I remember being so depleted, mad, and depressed that I took a hammer in my grandparent's basement and hit myself as hard as I could on my thigh. I still have the mark on my left thigh to prove it. The weight of feeling like I was never enough or that I would never be enough and feeling like a failure was a crushing blow. Failure was suffocating me and daily, I felt like I couldn't breathe and while I was alive, I felt as if I were walking dead. It felt like I was existing, merely surviving, instead of living. So, when trying to harm myself didn't work, I decided to take a more practical approach. I decided that I was just going to stab myself and die while everybody was sleep and they would find me in the morning when I didn't come upstairs for school. I still can remember holding the knife, crying, and feeling the weight of hopelessness and despair consuming me. All I wanted was to not feel this type of pain anymore. It was too much for me. It was in the darkest hour of my life that God stepped in. His hand reached down, stilled mine and I was unable to finish my intended plan. It was an indescribable feeling that I am so thankful for today because I couldn't go through with it. I remember the coolness of the knife pressing into my wrist. I could feel it against my skin, but something wouldn't allow me to cut my wrist. I started thinking about what my grandparents would say or how they would feel. How my mom and little sister would feel. Yes, I was tired of feeling like the scum of the Earth, but did I really want to put them through that pain? Did I really want to end my pain just to cause them an even greater one? Deep down, I knew I didn't.

I picked my Bible up and started looking through it. I remember seeing something at church that listed verses I could look up when I was having certain emotions. I was led to **Psalm 34:17** which states "When the righteous cry for help, the Lord hears, and rescues them from all their troubles." Also**, Deuteronomy 31:8,** "It is the Lord who goes before you. He will be with you; He will not fail you or forsake you. Do not fear or be dismayed." So, although I was hurting and wanting to end it all, God was there with me through it all. He saw that I was hurting, and He came to my rescue. **Jeremiah 29:11**, "For I know the plans that I have for you," declares the Lord, "plans to prosper you and not to harm you, plans to give you hope and a future." He saved me from a devil's hell. He stopped me in my tracks before I committed the biggest mistake of my life. He took the enemy's weapon right out of my hand and replaced it with His, the Bible. It is because of Him that I didn't go through with snuffing out my own life prematurely and put my family and friends through that unbearable pain of having to live life thinking they could have done something or should have done something to help me and having to live without me.

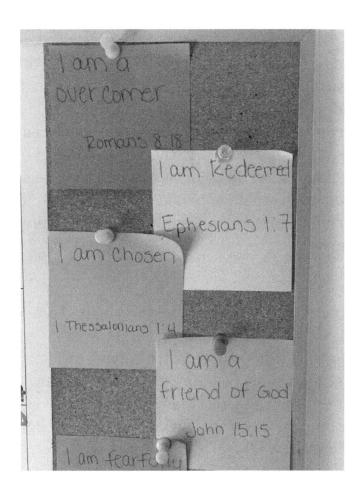

I've always struggled with depression and suicidal thoughts for majority of my life, but now I know that I am bigger than those thoughts. I am worth more than death to God. He has called me to be more than that. His power is so great inside of me and all I needed to do was access it. I just needed to tap into the source within me. So, I took a chance on Him, and life started to get better. I was believing the words that I was singing every Sunday. I was believing that He was the God that we sung about and sung to. Everything seemed good, too good to be true. Then in true life fashion, we get hit with a pandemic, I'm forced to stay home, and the world shuts down. Not to mention, the world being at civil unrest because of something that happened right in my apartment complex while my family and I were sleeping.

Breonna Taylor is killed in her home, just feet away from my own. I'll never forget what occurred just hours later after burying my daughter and my first Sunday School teacher. There's nothing scarier than waking up to gunshots coming from everywhere and you don't really know where all at the same time. It sounded like an explosion of fireworks. To have to prove to police that you are who you say you are and provide ID to prove that you live where you are telling them you live. To be patted down to make sure you don't have anything on you that can harm either yourself or the police. To have to place a "no comment" sign on your door so reporters can stop harassing and banging on your door for interview questions is traumatizing. The media has no respect for others. They clearly don't care that their invasion of privacy further triggers people when they have been traumatized by any incident. My precious child refused to sleep in her bedroom for a year in fear that she was going to be shot in her sleep like her neighbor was. She was so angry and confused as to why this happened or how it could even happen in the first place. I was unable to help her through this tragedy, so, I opted to put her in therapy to help her cope with her feelings and try to process what had happened. It was a lot, and although the pressure was intense at times, I stayed on course and continued to better my relationship with Jesus. As a creature of habit, it was extremely hard on me at first to get used to my new normal, but I eventually did and then what I have dubbed "the most challenging year of my life" occurred the following year. Year 2021.

The year of 2021 was no doubt my hardest year of life to date. I went through more than I thought was humanly possible starting January 6, 2021, when I got the news that my aunt Maria, the aunt I named my daughter Amaria after had passed. I was devastated, broken, and shocked all in one breath. It felt like I had been sucker-punched in the chest and all I could do was try to catch my breath and make sense of exactly what I was hearing. I eventually get through that only to lose another family member weeks later. You would think that was enough, but the cycle continued and would continue for the next 5 months with me losing my best friend, cousins, mother (step), grandmother, and it ended on my wedding anniversary with losing my younger brother. The entire year of 2021 I had lost one to two family members every month, except the month of July. I got a break and didn't lose anyone that month but then it picked back up again in August and my depression and suicidal thoughts intensified. The bed became my safe place and I no longer recognized who I was when I would get out of the bed to look at myself. I had hit an all-time low and was tired of life in general. This was a different feeling from the feelings that I felt in high school. These feelings were deeper, darker and I wasn't even sure how that was possible when I felt so low before, but it was true. I was tired of feeling like life wasn't fair to me and that terrible things only seemed to happen to me and nobody else, nobody understood, and nobody ever would. By then, I had been seeing a therapist as well as a psychiatrist because I knew something was wrong and off with me. I decided that the best option for me at that time was to continue therapy in order to become the best version of myself. I didn't want Amaria to have to grow up recovering from her childhood like I had to, so I was determined to do everything in my power to prevent that from happening to her. So, I decided to see a therapist who then referred me to a psychiatrist that wanted to put me on medicine to help me sleep better and make my anxiety and depression more manageable. Since they were the professionals in this area, I thought I would try their suggestion and I believed it to be helping, until it didn't. I had just lost my brother and I was still in a state of shock on top of losing a baby I didn't know I was pregnant with until after I had lost it. I started taking extra pills because I loved how it would allow me to sleep all day and see everyone that had been taken away from me in my dreams. Now I had found a form of addiction. As if my life wasn't already in great turmoil, I added another hurdle to it. This one, was possibly more deadly than the others. Because it was easy. It would be so easy to just empty the bottle and sleep forever and never have to experience another trauma in my life. So, I made the decision that I was going to take as many pills as I could so I could do just that, sleep forever.

I waited until my husband was sleeping and I started popping them in my mouth one by one as if I were eating Skittles. Hours later, I woke up.

Can you imagine the anger I felt to know that I had failed, yet again? I was so angry that it clearly didn't work so, I took more pills. I was positive that would do the job this time. Guess what? It didn't. I was devastated to wake up again hours later still alive. How blessed am I? How grateful am I today to get to be alive to say that God blocked it! I have come to the great realization that God has something powerful in store for me. If He has continued to protect me after many attempts, clearly there is a plan in His hand that He has been patiently waiting to unfold for my life. So, I eventually gave up trying. Praise God! It was simply His hand of protection that was keeping me safe, even from myself. He had so much in store for me and He needed me alive to be able to see and experience it all. Greater was coming for me and He would not let me go until I saw it.

It's been some time since all that went down and if I'm honest, I'm so glad that God didn't allow me to go through with any of those attempts to end my time on Earth prematurely. I think of all the things I'm doing and want to still do, and it makes me even more grateful that His hand was on my life because He knows that I am going to do massive things during my lifetime. There is no failure in Him, therefore there can't be any within me because He lives inside of me. I wish it hadn't of taken me so long to see that. However, now that I know, now that my vision is crystal clear, I know that as long as I'm breathing, I have a chance to be great. As long as I am breathing, I have the chance to be whole. As long as I am breathing, I have the chance to help someone else take their next breath also.

I've been told that God sees things in reverse because He knows how our lives are going to end and begin and He still loves us. He still gives us chance after chance to try to get it right and I'm thankful. Those nights could've gone a totally different way, someone else could be writing this testimony about me and urging others not to go down the same path, but I thank God I'm able to tell it for myself. God knew that I was going to hit several low points in my life, and He needed me to see that it wasn't my fault that I was raped and molested. I was more than what had happened to me. I am proud to say that I am no longer that scared little girl who was afraid to say anything out of fear of being talked about, ridiculed, or being called a liar. I feared that the most, that no one would believe me. God needed me to know and understand that there was absolutely no way that He could love me any less. Even with knowing that I would try to take my life, a life He had gifted to me, several times, I was still worth saving, I could still do and be everything that He had destined for me to be.

It is taking some time, but daily, I am healing and moving forward. I know it was nothing but the grace, mercy and reckless love of God that has kept me. I still have my days when the bad feelings want to creep in, but now I'm armed with the tools to get rid of those thoughts and get back to a better space. A lot of people feel several ways about seeing a therapist and while I chose to, others may feel that the best thing to do was pray about it. I respect others' decisions, but I had to take a different approach for me. Yes, I would pray and talk to God about how I was feeling but releasing those emotions and pent-up anguish from within me by talking to a therapist helped me majorly. It was the combination of the two that assisted me in seeing who I was. Getting back into church helped me tremendously, but therapy also helped me as well.

I also had found a church where the truth, the whole truth and nothing but the truth is constantly being preached. **Romans 10:14**, "How then shall they call on him in whom they have not believed? And how shall they believe in him of whom they have not heard? And how shall they hear without a preacher?" I have no choice but to believe what's being preached across the pulpit every Tuesday evening at 7:30pm and every Sunday afternoon at 2pm, when the Bible confirms everything that I'm hearing. It comforts me to be in a place that allows me to understand that I'm not alone in wanting to live a life unashamed about God and all He's done for me. I don't even want to imagine where my life would be if my aunt hadn't invited me to a service months ago. I would be dead. There is no doubt in my mind that I would have continued to rot and decay in my spirit if I had not found this place. If Jesus hadn't of lead me here. Since attending Greater Faith Louisville Central I've been baptized in Jesus' name and filled with the Holy Ghost! I haven't had a single suicidal thought, action, or depressing thought since then. I've also stopped taking all the medicine that was prescribed to me by my psychiatrist. So, you can't tell me that my God isn't a healer! Nobody can tell me that He can't do miracles, because I am a walking, living, breathing miracle in human form! I trust and believe that He can do anything but fail since I've seen it with my own eyes! God is so impressive and every time I think about everything that I have gone through and the fact that I am still here, I get overwhelmed. I cannot do anything but praise and worship Him because He looked at me, a complete mess, and said He wants me! He chose me! Flaws and all. All the ugly parts of me that people may or may not see, the real me that I used to hide behind my smile, He loves me past that. My stubbornness and rebellious ways, He looked down from Heaven and said, "I choose Courtney!"

Sometimes it is overwhelming that the creator of the entire universe recklessly, unconditionally, and irrevocably loves me. It makes me so happy! There is no way that I will ever keep my mouth shut about the things He's done in my life ever again. He deserves to be exalted. His goodness deserves to be shouted from mountaintops and valleys also because He is the same God in the valley and on the mountaintop. He does not change!

Knowing and unlearning all the lies that the enemy has told me over the years is a process, one that I intend to keep working at because I know I am destined for greater and that it's coming! All I can do is continue to fight. All I can do is to continue to stand on His word and His promises. They are ye and amen. He is not the God of empty or broken promises. He is the God of fulfilled ones! I can and will be everything that God says I shall and will be!

Hi, my name is Courtney, and I am an Overcomer!

Addiction:

The fact or condition of being addicted (physically and mentally dependent on a particular substance, unable to stop taking it without incurring adverse effects) to a particular substance, thing, or activity.

When we think of addiction our minds tend to automatically think about drugs and alcohol. However, addiction doesn't only include these substances but it includes many things. Addiction can include food, social media, pornography, sex, video games, nicotine, drugs, alcohol, etc. As the definition states, it includes substances, things and activities.

We tend to hold a microscope over certain addictions though, making them the scum of the Earth, while accepting others. Who are we to pretend that one is any greater than the other (1 John 5:17)?

We respond to the thought of addiction in the wrong manner. We are too busy trying to condemn addicts for their sin, when we should be trying to figure out how to help them come out of their sin. If we made the choice to nurture these individuals and welcome them into healing, how many more do you think would kick their habits?

If they were given the grace and mercy, they need to overcome their addiction, they would have a better chance at not becoming a statistic.

Upon researching on the internet, I found that there are approximately 20 million individuals in the United States with a substance use disorder. That is a lot of people. Those are a lot of souls that need to be reached and told that there is a way out. I get it. Not everyone takes heed to the advice of others. Not everyone will receive the message, but that doesn't mean you stop delivering the message. You never know who is listening to the sound of your voice and for that reason alone you have to always speak up and let people know that there is a way out. In 2020, there was nearly 92,000 people in the United States who died from a drug-involved overdose. This is a serious problem. How do we help solve it?

Instead of condemning people for the choices they have made or the damage they may have caused, we should try to get to the root of their issues and help them deal with those things so that they can make better choices in the future.

Prayer is also vital. We have to remember to pray for addicts, just as we pray for anything else. Our prayers should include their freedom from the trap that addiction has laid for them. They should include liberty for their souls. Prayer really does change things and it is the most powerful weapon we have against vile spirits like addiction.

Do you know someone who has an addiction problem? Have you ever been an addict yourself? If your answer is yes to either of those questions, then you know the turmoil that comes with it. You know the stress, the worry, and the fatigue that comes with dealing with an addict. This should drive us even more to want to do something to change the narrative.

If you've never been an addict or don't know anyone who is, this doesn't mean you shouldn't be involved. This means you have the awesome opportunity to get involved. You have a testimony of your own to share that can help them as well. Sharing your side of the story could help them to make a choice to cross the tracks to where you are. Don't be afraid to speak up.

The price we pay in being silent is another soul. That is too high a cost if you ask me. No one should have to pay a ransom with their life. However, I know someone who did. His name is Jesus Christ. He ransomed His life in hopes that we would get to have life for ourselves. He paid a debt that none of us could have and at times I'm sure we feel we don't even qualify to receive. If He could do that, the least we can do is share His goodness with someone else, especially an addict.

You would be surprised how many people really don't know God. This is why it is important that you become a walking billboard for who He is. Portray Him in a way that becomes magnetic to those around you. That when you are near, they are drawn to Him.

Be compassionate to people. Compassion goes a long way. I think too often we respond on auto-pilot. What I mean is that sometimes in situations where we really don't know what to say, we say what sounds right. For example, when people are having a hard time, it is a knee-jerk response for us to reply with "let me know if you need anything", without thinking. Sadly, I don't think we always mean this. We don't really say this thinking they will one day reach out and need something from us. We say this as a way to smooth over the conversation or end it completely. We should mean that. We should be genuine in offering our support and following through and being a support to our sisters and brothers in need. The same goes for when we respond with "praying for you", but then we never take their situation to the throne of God. I know not everyone does this, but I know it happens because I myself have been guilty of it in the past. I am now mindful of my language for that very reason. If I say "praying for you" to someone, I usually stop what I am doing and send up a short prayer then and later, I'll mention them again. Prayers don't have to be long and drawn out. This way, I am intentional about keeping my word and making sure God knows I care about the circumstances of others.

Addicts need your prayers. They need you to be men and women of your word. They need your grace, your love and your compassion. Be mindful of your safety at all times and don't be a pushover but also, don't turn the other cheek if you can be a help to someone. You aren't only helping them but you are helping their children, their spouses, their parents and all those affected by their addiction.

1 Peter 5:8 AMP Be sober (well balanced and self-disciplined), be alert and cautious at all times. That enemy of yours, the devil, prowls around like a roaring lion (fiercely hungry), seeking someone to devour.

James 1:12 AMP Blessed (happy, spiritually prosperous, favored by God) is the man who is steadfast under trial and perseveres when tempted; for when he has passed the test and been approved, he will receive the (victor's) crown of life which the Lord has promised to those who love Him.

James 4:7 AMP So submit (to the authority of) God. Resist the devil (stand firm against him) and he will flee from you.

Matthew 26:41 AMP Keep activity watching and praying that you may not come into temptation; the spirit is willing, but the body is weak."

1 Thessalonians 5:6-8 AMP So then let us not sleep (in spiritual indifference) as the rest (of the world does), but let us keep wide awake (alert and cautious) and let us be sober (self-controlled, calm, and wise). For those who sleep, sleep at night, and those who are drunk get drunk at night. But since we (believers) belong to the day, let us be sober, having put on the breastplate of faith and love, and as a helmet, the hope and confident assurance of salvation.

Amber Lynn Kerr was born and raised in Louisville Kentucky, where she spent most of her life. Amber is a wife and mother of 5 children. She has become an amazing mother who her children can look up to and she believes that ministry starts in her home. She resides in Bowling Green, KY. She and her husband, Mike, have been happily married for 5 years. They attend CrossPoint Tabernacle in Franklin Ky, where they have been members since 2019.

They both feel honored to be involved in many different ministries at CrossPoint. They love serving God, their church and others.

Amber and her husband lead a recovery intervention program at CrossPoint called Point of Hope. Together, they are dedicated and passionate about seeing others that struggle with addictions, overcome them through Jesus.

Amber is a strong, God-fearing woman who believes in the power of prayer. She has a powerful testimony, as told in this book, that witnesses to the amazing power of God! She is a fighter!

No matter what the enemy placed in her path, she never, ever allowed it to cause her to quit. She has been clean and sober since December 13, 2018. Her number one goal in life is to reach as many addicts as she can and share the gospel with them. She wants to be the willing conduit that God uses to show them that there is another way. To show others that this life is worth living and worth living more abundantly through Christ. Hell lost another one, but it is her mission to make sure hell loses many more. One can set a thousand and two, ten-thousand. She is ready to put the enemy to flight!

The Truth That Set Me Free

When I was asked to write this chapter, and after I decided this is what God wanted me to do, He spoke to me so clearly. He said, "Will you be brave enough to tell your whole truth to help point someone to me?" My whole truth. That's deep. Challenging, even. The part that stuck out the most was, 'to point someone to Him.' I thought on that and I realized what I wanted this chapter to be. I want my testimony to show the power of Jesus. I want my testimony to reflect His unending love for His children and that if He did it for me, He can certainly do it for anyone else and that would include you.

Not my will, but thy will be done (Luke 22:42). This chapter is going to be real. It is going to be one-hundred percent open and honest. My sincere prayer is that the words written on these pages will jump off and pierce someone's heart. I pray that you are able to feel my heart, soul and passion and that I can point another suffering person to the only one who can save them; Jesus. If not for another suffering person, I truly pray I can shine some light on and oppose the stereotype about "addicts." I pray that the words of my testimony challenge the perception of what some may believe about addicts. I pray that it is seen that they *are* human beings with deep pain, who are in *desperate* need of a savior. I hope that after reading this, you realize that **YOU** can love them back to life and lead them to Jesus. You and I were called to love people, so let's do just that. **LOVE PEOPLE!** I hope you enjoy hearing just how far Jesus has brought my family and I. It is truly by His grace and mercy that we still have breath in our bodies and that means that every breath is another chance to testify! This is my testimony.

My name is Amber Kerr, I am thirty-one years old. I have been married to my husband, Michael, for almost 5 years now and he is truly my best friend. We have been recovered from drug addiction since 2018. We have stood in the trenches together and we have also walked out of a life of sin, together. What you will come to know after reading this is that it wasn't always easy and many times it was messy. Through our walk with God, we have learned that our bond is special, and it is something that we cherish daily. We have learned to cherish it today more than yesterday and tomorrow more than today. Our passion in life is to help other people see that there is life after tragedy. We are burdened for souls that feel hopeless and worthless. It is not enough for us to experience the freedom that can only be found in Jesus, but we want to see others experience that same freedom. We want to tell everybody, about somebody, who can save anybody!

Together, Michael and I have a total of five children. We have four boys and one girl. For the sake of their privacy, I am choosing not to add their names into this book. We are blessed with amazing children. Michael and I started a painting company in 2020 and it has been blessed abundantly. We decided to name our company Renew Painting LLC. It was fitting because that is what our life has become, renewed in Jesus. When God told us to start our painting company, Michael was working out of town every week. Our children and I were seeing him only 8 days a month at the most. We knew that wasn't in the will of God. I began to pray that God would bring my husband home. One night at a prayer meeting God made me a promise. He said, "I'm not only going to bring him home, but I am going to triple his finances." We held on tight to that promise and we started Renew Painting. We began to pray that God would send us men that needed to be able to provide for their families. God has done just that; we now have a crew of men working with us. I am a stay-at-home mom, and I also help Michael run Renew Painting. I wouldn't trade my job for anything in the whole world. Ministry truly starts inside the home, and I get to serve my family every day. Jesus has continued to blow our minds. In the spiritual and in the natural. Later in this chapter I am going to discuss some of that, but first I am going to paint a picture of how life was before drugs.

I was born and raised in Louisville, Kentucky. I am the oldest of three siblings. I have a little sister who is two years younger than me and a little brother who is seventeen years younger than me. My parents divorced when I was seven years old and that was the beginning of my lineage of chaos. Being a child of a broken home comes with a lot of feelings, emotions and unfortunately it often comes with trauma. As a child, it is extremely difficult to deal with trauma. It is difficult enough to deal with trauma as an adult, so that proves the point of the difficulty that a child must experience when dealing with it. Sadly, divorce has become so normal in our society, that I believe we oftentimes fail to acknowledge that the children of these broken relationships and homes go through a "divorce process" themselves. I know I did. My world was flipped upside down overnight. Even though my parents had decided it was for the best that they separated, it was still difficult to grasp in my seven-year-old being. My childhood is a blur of both good and bad memories that seem to overlap. There are moments I wish I didn't remember and then there are others that I wish I could go back and experience all over again. My mother did the best she could with what she had, and she always made it happen, whatever "it" may have been in the moment. I have been tremendously blessed by her resilience, her strength and her determination.

With that being said, I cannot write this and let this opportunity pass by without giving two women in my life the recognition they deserve. The first being my grandmother. She taught me many things, but one thing I always remembered and held onto was that she taught me salvation as stated in Acts 2:38. She took me to a spirit-filled church, and she taught me the gospel of Jesus. She would always tell me, "Amber, you can trust in the Lord." My grandmother's love for the Lord has always inspired me. It reminds me of Proverbs 22:6 "Train up a child in the way he should go and when he is old, he will not depart from it." I am positive that it was some of her prayers, even from my young age, that kept me covered when I was desperately running around uncovering myself from God's grace. I believe that it was the protection of her prayers that had already gone before me to God covering my life while I was hellbent on destroying it. My grandmother's life echoes the Word of God, and I am forever grateful that she instilled the truth in me. Because in the end, it was in fact the truth that set me free!

The second woman is none other than my mother. She is the epitome of strength, dignity and perseverance. When life decided to throw everything but the kitchen sink at her, I never saw her fold. She may have been broken, but she never gave up. I'm sure she had some nights to herself where she cried, where she prayed and asked God to take the cup from her that she had been forced to drink. However, I never saw her weaknesses. I know that we all have them, and we usually deal with them in a quiet, secret place away from our kids as mothers because we don't want them to see our pain. We only want them to see our progress, our purpose and our love. Though life wasn't always easy for her, for any of us, for that matter, she still gave us her best. She instilled in me good morals, ethics and values. She taught me that if I failed, it was okay because I could always try again. She taught me to be strong, regardless of the circumstances facing me. We only truly lose when we quit. When we give up and stop trying, stop fighting, is when we lose.

My mother is the absolute best mother that I could have ever asked for. Though imperfect, as we all are, she has always been perfect for me. She has always been consistent and unwavering. Growing up, she had been the only constant in my life, and she is still always there for us. We never questioned whether mom would be there, we just knew. It was her strength that helped me through some of the toughest seasons of my life. Even when she lived in fear for my life, she refused to stop fighting for me. Champions, conquerors, victors only win because they refuse to stop fighting! My momma is now one of my very best friends. I cherish our relationship today and I thank God every day for her friendship.

There was never any rhyme or reason to the chaos that I always seemed to carry around with me. It seemed to track me down, follow me, and consume me from an early age. Just ask my mom! She'll tell you that I was wild, strong-willed, rebellious, difficult at times, though intelligent. She'll also tell you that I could be loving, caring and thoughtful. She'll tell you that I was adventurous and that I loved debates. That was a joke but somewhat true, nonetheless. I can remember that I wanted to be a lawyer or a doctor growing up. I remember that I loved to write. I love words and I love putting pen to paper, still to this day. That kind of made it easy for me to sit and write this chapter out for you all to read. Growing up I would write so that I could release the big emotions I felt on the inside that no one around me seemed to understand. Writing became an outlet for me to somewhat deal with the chaos within me. It was the truest form of therapy that I had at the time. Sometimes, if we leave all the chaos built up inside us and do nothing about it, it comes out in other forms. It comes out as attitude, disrespect, rebellion, outburst and far worse. That is exactly how my chaos began to manifest itself.

Chaos. A five-letter word that I thought summed up every fiber of my being. A word that gave way to a lifestyle that in many ways became comforting. Unhealthy, but comforting, nonetheless. Chaos. It grew with me. It fused its way into my DNA, consuming everything I touched. It became my normal, and my normal was everything except that. In my teenage years, I started to turn towards alternatives to deal with the chaos that had made its way into my life. I didn't know how to cope with the things that were happening in my life then, so I tried to find some sort of alternative. It started with seeking attention in any form I could find it, good or bad. The attention fed me for a while, until it didn't. I started using marijuana and pills by the time I was fifteen years old and life continued to spiral out of control. Before I knew it, my teen years were over, and I had been in bad relationship after bad relationship. I'm not sure what I saw in toxic guys, but I was attracted to that like a moth was to a flame. I am sure that it had to do with the war that was going on inside of me. The saying says birds of a feather flock together. Clearly, I wasn't free from toxicity myself. I assume that is what caused me to attach myself with others who were also toxic. If I settled for that and accepted that, then I didn't have to deal with or worry about anybody challenging me to change my own toxic behaviors. I was disastrous, destructive and it was clear I wasn't going to be making any changes anytime soon. I had two children by the time I was twenty years old. I was a baby having babies. How in the world would I be able to take care of children when I couldn't take care of myself? I had no idea what I was doing which resulted in putting my children off on their grandparents. At that time, I was in a very toxic and abusive relationship; I was on a merry go round of trauma and it was stacking up. It eventually stacked up to the point my life had become unmanageable. Even though I was unsure of how to care for them in this state, I knew where they would be safe.

To say that I hadn't even tried to be a mother to them would not be true. I did try. I tried with all my own might and clearly, in and of myself, I always came up short. Up until now my life had been a constant back and forth battle with my addiction. Being as how my grandmother made sure that I knew truth, I had tried to come back to it. After I had my second child, I decided to come back to my faith. One of my best friends was attending Greater Faith Church and she had invited me many times. What she didn't know is that I had went to that church with my father's side of the family as a child. I decided to go back to church. There, I became a faithful church-goer, I was given the opportunity to sing on their praise team, I had been a part of ministry. I was sober, I was trying to be a good mother to my babies. I had friends. I had family that didn't share the same blood as me. However, I never dealt with the inside like I needed to. I hadn't developed a strong prayer life that continued to grow along with me. I began to get complacent, and I allowed the enemy to trick me into believing that I was not worth His love. At the time, I believed that I could never be worthy of a godly life. Thoughts from the adversary started to plague my mind and so, I slowly started to slip back into the chaotic situations that I was used to. Chaos was the only place where I felt comfortable to be the failure, I had become accustomed to being. It was the only place I could be who I knew myself to be. Not who God said I was, but who my flesh believed I was. I thought I was unworthy to have a life that wasn't tied to chaos, and as a result I backslid. It wasn't because no one tried to help me, it wasn't because I was shunned or excluded. It wasn't because I wasn't loved because they absolutely loved me. It was me. I had strongholds that were yet to be broken.

Once again, I pulled my life down around me with my bare hands. Maybe it was the overwhelming pressure of the expectations that came with being the eldest child. Maybe it was the broken home I grew up in. Maybe it was because I perceived the world from a different set of lenses than most people. Pain will cause people to see things completely backwards. It causes our vision to be obscured as if we are living life looking through a terrible astigmatism. It very well could have been the trauma I suffered that I chose not to deal with. Maybe it was the stress from becoming a mother before I was mentally, emotionally or financially ready. Maybe it was because deep down, I chased the feeling of belonging, always needing others approval and acceptance. Maybe it was the crippling fear of never being good enough. Maybe it was because I was just plain hardheaded, and I had become the definition and the epitome of chaos. Then again, maybe, just maybe there was a spiritual battle for my soul happening from the moment I took my first breath. But whatever the reason, by the age of 25 I was a full-blown heroin IV user. For years, I continued to search out different ways to mask what I was dealing with on the inside. My life had quickly become shattered in a million pieces on the ground around me. I was like a tornado that ripped through every life I encountered. Bringing the wreckage of my own life into their front yards. No invite, no welcome party, just chaos. It continued to live within me and it was growing bigger and meaner every single day. I was broken. I was angry. I was hurting. I was lost. In true vagabond fashion I aimlessly wandered through life. There was no physical solution to my spiritual problem. However, I was determined to find one.

Trap houses, night clubs, jails and institutions were no longer something that I had seen in movies but it had quickly become my reality. My reality. It was real. It was so real. Somewhere between being "dope sick", needing another fix and my next high, I would have moments of clarity where I would want to be sober. Somewhere between couch surfing and sleeping on park benches, I would yearn to get my life on track and be a better person, a better daughter, a better mother, a better sister and a better friend. My life consisted of "one day" statements and "tomorrow's". "Tomorrow, I'm going to get clean. I'll go to rehab, tomorrow. One day, I'm going to get off the streets. One day, I'm going to take this needle out of my arm and live for God. One day, I'm going to be a wife and a mom." Each one day, turned into another day and it seemed as if that day was so far out of reach. It felt as if tomorrow would never actually come. The sad reality of these statements was that I never doubted them. Every time I made those statements, I really believed myself when I said them. I believed it, with every fiber of my being because deep down I really wished I could get clean and remain that way. I am positive that it was my ability to believe those things that eventually helped turn my life around. Remember, earlier I mentioned that one passage of scripture, train up a child. I was in a season of straying, but eventually I had to find my way because I had been a child who was trained up; therefore, I could not fully depart. Could I?

I truly believe that there is a common misconception some people have about addicts that they "want" to be that way. Can I challenge that belief for a moment? That stereotype is completely false. Take it from someone who lived a life full of addiction for many years. I can attest that stereotype couldn't be any farther from the truth. I can promise you no one ever says, 'I think I'm going to get addicted to drugs and ruin my life when I grow up!' It doesn't happen like that. Most of us had real hopes, dreams, and ambitions. Sure, some of us may have become products of our environments but for most recovered addicts I talk with, they all say similar things. "I wanted to be a doctor, lawyer, teacher, mother, father, wife, husband." Drugs slowly try to steal our futures and the futures of everyone affected by this disgusting disease.

The truth is, I hated myself. I hated what I had become and more importantly I hated what I had done to myself and so many others around me. I was slowly killing myself and I was causing harm to everyone in my path without even wanting to. I didn't want to hurt anyone; it just came with the lifestyle. I didn't want to push everything and everyone away for one more fix. I didn't want to keep destroying my life and the lives of everyone who loved me, especially my kids. I didn't want to abandon my children for drugs, but I did, time and time again. Addiction hurts the addict, but even more, it also destroys those who love them.

I wanted to be a mother to my children, but I didn't know how. I wanted to do something with my life. I wanted to be a wife. Heroin wouldn't let me. Everything I "wanted" to be in life at the time seemed so unrealistic. How was a needle junkie like me going to be anything other than that? Besides, I knew that few of us ever really made it out and if we did, it wasn't for long. This is where I found comfort in chaos. There's that five-letter word again. It continued to mold my life a little more with each needle I stuck in my arm.

After living in addiction for so long, I knew what to expect, I knew how to deal with it and I had become comfortable living in it. I'm not sure if comfortable is the correct term to use, because it was more like I became completely numb to my reality. I thought that heroin was the only way to deal with the constant chaos in my mind. I thought heroin "fixed" me, even if it was for a short moment. I thought heroin was the answer to the mental battle I faced. When I used heroin, I didn't feel like I wanted to crawl out of my skin, every single day. By 2017, I had been in and out of jail and rehab more times than I can probably remember. I had a rap sheet a mile long and I was guilty. Guilty of allowing chaos to control me. I was guilty of giving my addiction everything worthwhile in life. Every couple of months I would find myself detoxing on a cold concrete floor in an orange jumpsuit in Louisville Metro Department of Corrections. It never got any easier but I was no stranger to that concrete floor. I had grown accustomed to it.

I met my husband in 2016. We got married and had a baby in September of 2017. I became pregnant with our son in the center of my addiction. My doctor eventually called me out on my drug use and offered me help. They said they could medically detox me and place me on a maintenance medication called subutex or suboxone. This meant that our baby was at risk of being born addicted, but it also meant that if I did not go on that medication our baby could have lost his life before it ever began. We chose the medication route and unfortunately our son was born addicted. He had to be medically detoxed.

I can still remember the sounds of the NICU machines, the IVs and monitors attached to my baby. I was faced with a mess that I created. The sad part was that I thought I was really hiding it from everyone. As if they did not know what I had done. Ashamed of myself and feeling defeated, I was determined to do it right this time. I tried with all my might to stay on the right path but the problem was I did not deal with the pain I carried around with me. Maintenance medication may work for some but for me it led me back to the inevitable, my addiction to heroin. It was as if it was just lying dormant waiting to distract me at the right time.

Sure enough, it did just that. Once again, I failed! Being in active addiction is like being on an endless roller coaster and you never know when it will end. You just hold on for dear life and hope that you live to tell about it. If I am being honest, there were days I felt a sick peace with the idea of not living to tell about it. If that meant the vicious cycle would finally end, so be it. Heroin took me past the point of suicidal. There were times before I would get high that I would hope it would be the last needle I ever pushed into my arm. There were times I wished I didn't wake up because when I did it meant I would have to chase down my next fix again. My addiction had been an awful, painful, tormenting cycle of getting clean only to relapse. I would be clean just long enough to start building a decent life and then all at once, in a blink of an eye, I would pull it all down around me with my bare hands, again.

Insanity? Absolutely.

Normal? Maybe not for you, but it was for me.

Eventually, my pain was so great that I couldn't numb it anymore. The pain rang so loudly in my mind that I just knew I was going crazy. I cannot even find the words to adequately explain the mental agony my addiction brought me. I have tears rolling down my face as I am typing this because it was that exact pain, that led me to the most beautiful life. Pain that I later decided I was going to be strong enough to turn into purpose.

My addiction took me further than I ever wanted to go, kept me longer than I ever wanted to stay, and it cost me more than I ever wanted to pay. Which brings me to this specific event in my life, that up until this moment, I have never shared in detail. I'm often asked what was it that made you stop? What was the last straw? I didn't ever have an answer until I was asked to write this. I had always given a generic version of what I thought was the last straw.

To understand what got me to that point, first I am going to take you back to that day that Jesus intervened. I do not say that lightly either, after reading this it will be clear as day that it could have only been Jesus. In September of 2018, my husband and I had relapsed, again. In just 2 short months, we lost everything. Our jobs, our son, our sanity, our home, all the weight we gained being sober, and we were about to lose our car. Soon, we were going to lose each other. It was inevitable. We knew that if we didn't get clean and sober, we were going to lose our lives to heroin. Our life was quickly being ripped apart again and we were to blame.

In this two-month timespan, we both overdosed more than a handful of times. Which ended in EMS having to administer a lifesaving drug called Narcan. For those that don't know what Narcan does, it reverses the side effects of opioids and causes your body to "wake up." Unfortunately, it doesn't save everyone but it has given countless second, third and fourth chances to those of us whose lives were wrecked by opioids. I can look back over my life and see that the only reason Mike and I still have breath in our body is because Jesus said so. There is no other explanation. Neither of us should be alive today. But, God!

Things were worse than they had ever been. They say it gets worse before it gets better, and it is true. It always gets worse. Only this time, it was agonizing, tormenting pain. It was December 2, 2018 and I will never forget this day. My husband was so tired. He was so done living that way. For him, enough was enough.

I watched him call around to rehabs, pleading with them to give him a bed. He was relentless and I was of no help. The entire time I kept saying things like, "Mike I'm not ready, I'm not going with you." "How are you just going to leave me out here like this?" I was downright hateful and discouraging. Nothing that came out of my mouth that day was helpful. His reply was simple, matter of fact, and to the point. He said, "Amber, I am going to rehab. I am going to get clean, and I am going to do it with or without you."

My heart sank. He was serious. He finally got the call that a rehab in Elizabethtown had a bed for him. I watched my husband pack his bag. You would think that I would want to go with him, but I did not. I refused. I was not going to fight through withdrawals only to relapse again in 6 months. My heart was cold as ice. I watched him walk out the door without a single emotion and as cold as my heart was, I was on a mission of pure destruction from that moment on. I remember being completely shut off from any form of sanity. There was no rhyme or reason to my madness.

Still to this day, I thank God for that moment of hope my husband grabbed ahold of. I thank God for putting a burning desire to be clean and sober on the inside of him in what seemed like an instant. The determination I saw in his eyes that day is the same look of determination in his eyes today. He fights to live for God like no one I have ever seen. He makes sure that he gives Jesus more than he gave his addiction. It is so powerful to see someone, especially your person, giving God everything, they have. Thankful and grateful can't even begin to scratch the surface to describe the emotions I have right now about what God has brought us from.

My husband is one of the most humble, inspiring men I know. God put a fire on the inside of him that day that has not gone out since. There is a light that has continued to burn for Christ, shining within him for all the world to see. Today, I understand that my husband stepped out with faith neither of us knew was within him and he began to lead our home for the very first time that day. God put a desire in him to fight and with Mike's obedience, the Lord put a plan into motion for both of our lives and the lives of our children without us even knowing it. A song says, "Even when I can't see it, you're working. Even when I don't feel it, you're working. You never stop, you never stop working." Jesus truly is the way maker. Michael decided to go before me, knowing in that moment, that he may never see me again. He left, knowing heroin may kill me. Yet he still went with the faith of a mustard seed that I would eventually follow him. His faith inspires me every day and I am beyond grateful to call him, mine.

Later that day after Michael left for rehab, I had started to go into withdrawals. After prolonged IV heroin use, you start to get physically sick after a couple of hours from your last use. It was a cold night, colder than I had ever experienced before. I guess it just felt freezing to me as I was walking to my car because my teeth chattered uncontrollably. I had no winter jacket; I was wearing a dirty sweatshirt with matching sweatpants that I hadn't changed in a week and hadn't eaten in just as long. I was roughly one hundred and seven pounds and I'm sure I am being generous. Just to put my weight into perspective, I am five foot seven. The clothes I had on me were a size small and they were falling off.

It was as if I could smell disaster lingering in the air. I had felt this way before, many times, the disparity, the anger, the loneliness, that lump that welled up inside my throat as I fought back tears.

As I slipped into my car, I gripped the steering wheel so tight I am surprised that I didn't disconnect it from the vehicle. I laid my head back on the headrest with tears flowing down my face and for the first time in my whole life, I thought that there had to be more to life than that. Although I really didn't know how to do anything other than what I was about to do.

I knew I was about to take off to find another fix. I had to; it was a necessity. The withdrawals were so bad I could barely function. I felt every muscle in my body tense up, my hands were sweating, my legs were so restless. I was nauseous and my body hurt so bad. I felt as if my body was not in control of itself. Some might say, why didn't you call someone? I couldn't. I had no one to call. This is what addiction does, it rips everything and everyone away from you. You are eventually left alone with the tormenting thoughts that haunt your mind.

There were so many thoughts swirling in my mind that I could only seem to make sense of one, and that was "I have to get well." As I drove to that horrendous house that I once swore I would never go to again, I was thinking 'not again.' I got out of the car, shaking, walked up to the door and went inside. I got what I needed and then asked to use the bathroom. I remember sitting on the bathroom floor, crying, as I did what I always did. Though this time was different, I was so tired. Weary. That's what I was. I was weary from living like that, but I didn't know how to live any other way.

I thought that was it; that had become my life and I truly believed there was no way out. I had no idea that I didn't have to be that way. I had no clue that there was a real and lasting solution to my drug problem. Again, I found comfort in chaos. The withdrawals faded and the pain was quieted but I still felt empty. I still felt hopeless and worthless. I opened my mouth and said, "God if you really love me, please take me or get me out of this."

In that moment, sitting on that bathroom floor in a puddle of my own tears, I managed to mumble the sincerest plea to the Lord in almost 5 years. It wasn't one of those foxhole prayers that I would say while I was sitting in jail that went something like - 'God if you get me out of this, I'll do that.' It was a real and sincere prayer. I really was sick and tired of living like that. If Michael could believe that he could be free, so could I. The God I serve works miracles in the midst of a sincere cry for help. I believe with every part of me that at that exact moment, God reached down and began to place things in order. He began to rearrange some things, set some things into motion, shut some doors and open some others. After living out my testimony, I can clearly see that there is no other way I made it out alive. I should have died a thousand times, but God! But, for the grace of God, there go I.

The next 48 hours are still a blur. I have little to no recollection of what took place, where I went, how I got there or anything. It is the scariest thing to think about or admit. Still to this day, I am left with the questions, where did I go? What did I do? It is gut wrenching to think about. The only thing I remember is that on December 4th, 2018, I came to in a pool of sweat and I was freezing cold. I felt all the effects from the withdrawals. The body aches, the chills, the cold sweats, the nausea, the stomach pain, the anxiety, and depression. I felt as if at any moment I could physically crawl out of my skin. I looked around the room and thought to myself, "where am I"? I got up; the room was spinning. I opened the door, walked down the hall. Every step I took I felt as if I would collapse, every part of my body ached, even the hairs on my arms were sore. My body was weak, my mind was racing. Through very blurred and distorted vision, a nurse was walking towards me. I demanded to know where I was. How had I gotten here?

She told me I was in a drug rehabilitation center in Elizabethtown KY. I immediately went into fight or flight mode. I was confused, I was angry, I was dope sick and that combination was like putting a wild animal in a cage. I demanded to know how I got there, who signed me in there and why? I mean as if the why wasn't glaring and obvious, I needed help and deep down I knew that. After they were able to calm me down, they took me to the intake office where they answered all my questions. I had gotten a ride there with my sister, I signed myself in and they told me that I sounded desperate for a bed on the phone. I called them. I couldn't believe it.

Desperate? I don't remember that. I barely remember being with my sister, let alone the drive up there. It was becoming clearer that in the time between what I did remember and then, I was in a black out. That should have woken me up right then and there, but it didn't. I vividly remember that I begged the sweet woman doing my intake paperwork to give me my phone back. They had taken it the night I came in. I was crying and screaming at her to just give me my phone and let me go because "she just didn't understand

and that people like me don't make it out, we die." She stood her ground and refused to give me my phone. I was so angry but deep down in the innermost part of my being, my soul was screaming for someone to save me from myself. What I thought would be just one more person that was just going to cave and give up on me, was really a person who had decided that I was worth fighting for. What I thought was a person who didn't understand, really did understand.

I truly believe that God used her to stop me. God used her to show me that I was worth fighting for, that I was worth believing in, and that no matter how bad I had become that I was worth sobriety. She didn't judge me, instead she offered one thing that has stuck with me, compassion. She sat with me as I was curled up in a ball in her office floor, with tears flowing from her eyes, she told me a story that confirmed that she understood me. She told me that I was stronger than I thought I was and that I could do this. She gave me more hope that day than she'll ever know. So, I stayed. I completed rehab and I have been clean ever since. Today, I thank God that I don't remember what happened before I went to rehab, and I thank God for His hand of protection on my life. I think God put me in a spiritual coma in order to save me. In order to calm the chaos, I was so accustomed to. He cared enough to keep me in a cocoon of grace while He worked a plan to save my life.

When I take the time to look back on my life, there is no doubt that Jesus has always been in the details. The small intricate details, that many times, we overlook. The details that to us make no sense. God doesn't have to make sense, He makes miracles. I have learned that when we cannot seem to find God anywhere else, we can find Him in the details of our lives. There was a reason that I did not remember getting to rehab. There is a reason God chose to do it that way. He knows me better than I know myself and He knows what is best for me. He knew I would not go to rehab without divine intervention, and I am forever grateful that He intervened.

I wish I could tell you this is where I came back to Jesus, but unfortunately, I had to go through a little more pain before I went to an altar of repentance. Remember earlier when I said God had begun to open some doors and close some other ones? While I was in rehab, I was faced with having to find a place to live with my youngest child. My mother told me that I needed to take my son back. She was already raising my other two boys. Through tears she told me that she felt like if I didn't have another chance at being a mother that she may lose her child forever. I am forever grateful for that second chance, because it forced me to grow up. It awakened something in me that gave me a reason to live. It gave me a reason to remain sober, for the sake of all my children.

I began to call around and look for sober living facilities that would allow me to bring my child with me. What I quickly learned is that there is a lack of resources for mothers trying to remain sober who still have custody of their children. Almost every long-term treatment center I called, no children could come with me and the ones that could, were full. Every single door shut, except for one, in Bowling Green KY. Another example of God's hands being in the details. Bowling Green was two and a half hours away from everything that was once so toxic to me. My son and I headed to Bowling Green, together. Michael eventually found a sober living house there as well. Isn't it just like God to remove us from one environment to introduce us to a land that will flow with milk and honey for our lives? I thank God for His ordered steps.

On this new journey, I learned so much about being a mother. The house I went through was a six-to-eighteen-month program and I successfully completed it, in nine months. It was one of the most amazing things that has ever happened to me. I often refer to it as "mommy boot camp," because to me that is exactly what it is. It is a program that gives structure to both mother and child. They were able to combine parenting classes, recovery intervention, therapy and some behavior modification while reintroducing a mother to the workforce. Meaning, they set you up to be able to succeed if you put in the work. I had a decision to make, to change or stay the same. Staying the same was far scarier than the pain it was going to take to change and for me, change, is always painful.

There, I was encouraged to deal with childhood traumas that I've never spoken about. It helped me to do intense therapy work on my inner self and it allowed me to be a mother at the same time. Trying to heal and be the mother my child needed was by far the hardest thing I have ever done, but it was necessary. It showed me two things; one, that I CAN do anything I set my mind to and two; that I DO have the ability to persevere and grow through uncomfortable situations. I learned that growth and comfort cannot co-exist. It takes being uncomfortable to grow in ANY situation in life. I have come to embrace uncomfortable seasons even today, because I know it is in those moments that I grow the most. It is a reminder that I am growing and if I am growing that means I am becoming better than I was the day before. I know that if I ever get complacent, history could repeat itself.

Shortly before completing the program, I will never forget the pain my husband and I were feeling, and we were sober as could be. Just because we were clean and sober does not mean that we were exempt from pain, trials, and hard situations. Life still shows up regardless of if we are sober or not. We quickly learned that we could become just as miserable sober as we were getting high. I wish I would've known that there are no physical solutions to spiritual problems long ago. I could have kept many people from experiencing so much unnecessary pain a long time ago. I had a spiritual problem. I was spiritually dead therefore being clean and sober wasn't the answer to every problem I had.

After completing the program, Michael and I moved in together, we reunited as a family. We both had to figure out how to navigate life as a married couple, sober. We were both crippled with shame, guilt, remorse, anger and unforgiveness that took root as bitterness. All those emotions were being lashed out towards one another causing a chaotic situation. Not to mention, I had just found out that I was pregnant with our daughter. All the changes we were going through as a family and as individuals was probably a good indicator that we needed help to figure everything out. We had no idea how to live life without the use of a substance. We had no idea how to deal with ourselves let alone, each other.

We both knew we were missing something in our life, but we didn't know what. We prayed little prayers here and there, but that hardly counted for a relationship with our Creator. As miserable as we had both become, we began to toy around with the idea of just giving up and going back to what we knew. That seemed like the only thing we could do. It was the only thing we seemed to be successful at. Besides, it was really the only thing we'd ever done before; we would just give up when things got hard. We would always give up right before the miracle happened. We thought, why change now?

After a rough day and little sleep because of the chaos that once again tried to find its way into our lives, I had another moment of clarity. I was sitting on our porch to our new home, mind racing and I heard a still small voice say, "the truth will set you free." THE TRUTH. I knew truth. I knew the power that was found in true freedom. I had experienced it for myself. My mind became flooded with different scriptures like Acts 2:38, and Jeremiah 29:11.

For a week straight, I felt God calling me, I felt Him drawing me, every minute of every day. I would lay awake at night and think about it. Every time I got on social media, I would see things about Jesus. There was a stirring happening in my spirit until I couldn't take it anymore. I knew I had to get back to a spirit-filled church. A truth preaching church.

I asked my mom where some Apostolic churches were in my area and she gave me only one - Crosspoint Tabernacle in Franklin KY. The week after that my mom and I went to a bridal shower for my cousin at that church. They were all so welcoming and kind. As I sat there, seeing everyone laughing, having fun, and living free, I remember thinking to myself, 'I want what they have.' As I sat there in silence, it took almost everything I had in me not to cry. I knew I was lost. I was secretly being convicted. I knew better. I knew exactly why everyone had genuine joy. I told my husband about Crosspoint and told him that I think we should try it out. He was reluctant and he proceeded to tell me that we had tried church before. I remember saying, but we haven't tried truth. At this point we were both desperate enough for a solution. We weren't using drugs, but we weren't happy. We weren't living life the way that God had intended for us to live it. Happy, joyous, and free. Free, with liberty and peace in our minds and hearts.

We still had chains that no one could see. At that time, I knew we were eternally homeless, and I knew that we didn't need to go to just any church. We needed a Jesus name church. We needed salvation as it's clearly stated in Acts 2:38. We honestly had nothing to lose by trying so he agreed. I knew that I had to get us there. I had to touch the hem of Jesus' garment. I knew that if I could just get close enough to the altar and touch Jesus- He would restore my family because chains break at the weight of His glory. I knew He could break our chains; He could set us free. I was desperate enough for a change that I would have crawled there if I had too. I knew that this one step would not just change us, but it would drastically change the course of our life and our children's lives for generations to come.

It was August 2019, we walked into a church service at Crosspoint Tabernacle for the very first time. Miracles are in this place and I'm not just saying that because it's my church home. I am saying that because it is absolutely the truth. The truth that set us free, is still the same truth that keeps us free today. When my needle met the cross. When my addiction met mercy. When my faults, failures and mistakes met grace and my bondage met freedom, life started to look a little different. When we met Jesus, everything changed because Jesus changes everything.

I was so scared that we would be met with judgment and ridicule for the life that we had lived, but fear is a liar. We were met by a group of people with open arms. We were met there with people that showed us that we were worth fighting for. They saw something in us that we did not see in ourselves. They chose to love us when we were unlovable. They chose to rally around us and fight hell for us and they still stand with us today. I wish I could adequately describe the love that was poured out onto my husband and I when we walked in. Crosspoint Tabernacle taught me what the true definition of love is. Niagara Falls doesn't have enough water to equate to the magnitude of love that these people poured on us. We didn't just find friends, we found family.

It reminds me of the prodigal son returning from the parable in the book of Luke. They didn't judge us, they didn't shame us, instead they met us with open arms and said welcome home. They celebrated us being there. We were home. They loved us back to life in every way possible.

Without our Pastor and his wife, without the true friendships we have found in this place, I do not know where we would be. There is no perfect church, but to us, there is no place like Crosspoint. It was in this place, that my husband and I began a whole new journey together. We took the first step to let Jesus into the life that we were building together, and because of that life as we had known it to be, changed.

We made up our mind that we were going to be faithful to the house of God. We decided to give it everything we had. How could we not after we had given addiction so much of us? It was only right that we would do the same, even more, for God. We were all in from the start. Not because we are special in any way, but we knew that we had to try with all our might. Our lives really depended on it. We knew we had to be all in or all out. There wasn't any living on the fence with God. We are living, breathing proof that if you want to be used by God, you can be! There is nothing stopping you from having the things of God, except yourself, except your will. Were we perfect? Not at all. Far from it even. Sometimes it was messy, but we were willing. We were willing to learn, we were willing to try, and we were willing to believe in the truth that set us free. We were willing to be vulnerable and real. We were willing to trade our will for His. Today, we are still just as willing to learn, and we are just as determined to grow because we cannot afford to become stagnant.

We watched our pastor and his wife and the other leaders in our church, we watched how they did things. We watched how they lived, and we watched how they operated. We did exactly what they did. It may sound a little juvenile, but when my pastor's wife raised her hand to worship, I did too. When my pastor's wife picked up one of her children, I did too. I did everything she did and still to this day I watch her to learn from her. She has this amazing ability to tell you like it is, while showing you like it is. You may ask why I still watch her, and the answer is simple, because she is the kind of leader, mother, wife, and friend that I want to be. I want to always learn from her because I want the spiritual life she lives. The godly woman, mother, and wife I am today is because she showed me how and she still shows me how. I watch her because she is the example God has blessed me with to follow. No matter how much I mature spiritually, I always want to remain teachable, humble, and correctable. If not, I am afraid it will be the easiest, quickest trip back to defeat and despair and that is not an option at this point in my life.

We submitted ourselves to our pastor's authority and leadership. We gave him the chance to pastor us. We allowed him and his wife to speak into our lives and we allowed them to develop us into leaders. They built a relationship with us, and because of that we were able to trust them. Trust is huge for all of us, especially people with trauma. Consistency is also. We were not able to trust anyone without first seeing that they were consistent. Pastor Stephen and Ashley Perry are two of the most consistent human beings that I have ever met. They are selfless, dedicated, and loving. They are true, humble, and genuine. Their actions showed us that. They saw something in us that we did not see in ourselves, and they continue to see something in us that we don't see. They spoke vision over our lives and continue to do so. They taught us that giving up is never an option. They cover us, they pray for us and with us, they love us, they fight for us.

If you are new to your walk with Jesus, you NEED a covering. Hear me and hear me well. You need a pastor. If you aren't new to your walk with Jesus, you still NEED a covering. You still need a pastor. We need someone that will watch out for our souls. We need people in our life that refuse to let the enemy take us out. It is not just a suggestion that the bible refers to, it is scripture to have a pastor and to listen to that pastor. It is not enough to just have a pastor; you must also allow them to pastor you. Know this. When deception is afoot, and the enemy is sending wolves into your camp - you will be thankful for a watchman on the wall. When you are too blind to see the edge of the cliff and you have a shepherd to say, stop, you're going too far, there is danger ahead, you'll be grateful. It is imperative that you have a true man of God in your life. It is not punishment, it is protection. It is not tyranny, it is safety.

We have learned that you cannot have a godly life without true submission. As a wife, I must be submitted to my husband and to God. As the head of our household, he must remain submitted to God. Together, we must stay submitted to our leadership; our pastor and his wife. Submission is necessary, there is no way around it. Sometimes, the word no, has God's goodness written all over it, and we must have people in our lives that are not afraid to tell us no. We must have leaders in our lives that aren't afraid of our temper tantrums. We must have leaders who will refuse to sugarcoat anything for the sake of our souls.

I look back over my life and it is surreal that I have made it this far. It is even more surreal that my husband and I have made it this far together. Statistically, him and I shouldn't be sober, we shouldn't have our children, we shouldn't be business owners. We shouldn't be living for God. We shouldn't be more blessed than we have ever been before in our lives. We deserve to have lost our minds a long time ago. We deserve to have lost one another to death or divorce. We should have tombstones with our names on it saturated with the tears of the people who loved us beyond addiction. But when I think of the goodness of Jesus and all that He has done for me, I cannot help but to celebrate. I cannot help but to shout, hallelujah! I cannot help but to become undignified in my worship, because I have a song that the angels cannot sing. It is the song of redemption. God said we didn't deserve death, we didn't deserve divorce, we didn't deserve insanity. He went to a cross two thousand years ago so that we could receive peace, liberty, freedom, and a chance to get it right!

Jesus is a statistic breaker. He is the God of the impossible. This does not mean that everything became perfect overnight. Quite honestly, it was the opposite. It was a spiritual battle. Anyone who has decided to live for God knows that you end up with a bigger target on your back. The enemy becomes furious when you don't give up, you don't quit, you don't curse God and die like Job's wife tried to coax him into doing. When you make the decision to live for God you must be ready for battle. You must be ready to put armor on and stand flatfooted, toe to toe with whatever the enemy throws your way. So, we had to fight for the life that we wanted to live and when I say fight, I literally mean fight.

If it had not been for the Lord who was on our side, I don't know where we would be. I see people come to Jesus expecting for a microwave response from Him. Let me explain what I mean by that - all too often I see people that come to Jesus expecting for an immediate turn around in their situation without them having to do anything at all. They treat God as if He is some genie in a bottle and He's just not. Like with everything else in life, there is a process. Now, don't get me wrong, God does do some expedient works. However, we must continue to work at dying to our flesh daily, to continue to abide inside of the grace that He has given to us, even in the quick works that He performs for us. The work He did for us though, was slow and meticulously. It was a crock pot type of work. This is what we needed. It was what was best for us, and nobody knew what was best for us more than God.

I know that is probably an unpopular opinion and that's okay. I know that my God can do exceedingly, abundantly, above all that I could ask or think, and I also know that there is nothing that He cannot do, outside of failing. However, I know what it took to walk out of our life that was riddled with sin. When you have lived a life of shame, regret, and immoral compromise, it is going to take work. It is going to take time to repair the destruction and havoc you have wreaked on your life. First, it takes a made-up mind to do something different and then it takes work. It takes work to unlearn toxic behaviors. It takes work to do the inner work. We had to be willing to put in the work. We had to want to change. We had to make up in our minds to be sold out for Jesus.

I believe that Jesus does what we cannot do for ourselves, but He will not do what we can do for ourselves. I never want to portray my life or my walk with God as an elaborate fairy-tale. It is not. Living for God has allowed us to live life more abundantly. God has done more for us than anything I could have ever imagined. But understand this, it took intense work to climb out of a life of sin. It took obedience, passion, resilience, determination, and supernatural strength to even take the first step to climb out of the pit we had found ourselves in. It takes those same ingredients to stay out of that same pit as well.

Looking at our life today, as it is now, some think we just woke up one day, decided we were finished with that lifestyle, and lived happily ever after. To be blunt, this isn't Disney. People do not see the times we thought our marriage would not make it, the times we had to fight through the physical craving to pick up a needle or a bottle when things got tough. People do not see how we had to unlearn previous behaviors in order to learn to handle life differently. The substances that allowed us to go numb and cope were no longer an option. We had to learn to simultaneously fight our physical desire and the spiritual attack on our mind telling us we would never be anything but failures. We had to train our minds to think different. We had to speak truth over the lies that the enemy tried to get us to believe.

Matthew 19:26 says, Jesus looked at them and said, "With man this is impossible, but with God all things are possible." That scripture sums it up. What was impossible for us became possible with God. He is the God who makes impossibilities possible. We have seen God move in the details of our life repeatedly. Today, Michael and I are a team, a good team. Dare I say a great team! We help each other, we listen to one another, not just to respond but to receive what the other is saying. We genuinely care for one another. Not just our physical bodies, but our spiritual ones. When one of us is off, the other one helps pick the other up. Is our marriage perfect? Not at all. Whose is? However, I wouldn't trade the life we live today for anything in this whole world.

We have been reunited with all of our children. Situations that seemed impossible, became possible. Jesus has restored relationships within our families that we never thought could be repaired. We never ever thought we would be business owners, and that it would be blessed beyond what we deserve. We have stability and self-discipline today. Jesus has continued to take us from glory to glory. As we grow in Christ, we go to deeper levels with Him. Only Jesus can take two junkies and place their feet upon a rock that would take them higher than they ever dreamed of being. He picked us up and turned us around. We now get to share with others who are suffering that there is hope and that hope is only found in Jesus.

Together we are laying a foundation of truth for our babies to stand on. Jesus has broken generational curses of addiction and trauma. Mike and I both agree, it stops with us. We fight daily to take a stand against the devil who wants nothing more than to destroy our children. We have declared, not in this house, not with our babies! As for us and our household, we will serve the Lord! All the we have witnessed including our own, tells us one thing, that He is too good to not believe. He is too good to not be true. He is the truth that set us free and miracles continues to keep us free. We have overcome by the blood of the lamb and the word of our testimony!

The most important thing that I believe I have gained is a sound mind. I am no longer bound by the tormenting thoughts that held me captive in my own mind. I'm a firm believer that an idle mind is the enemy's playground. We must guard our minds. My husband and I are mentally capable of making sound, reasonable and disciplined decisions today. That wasn't always the case. Above all things, we have a peace that surpasses all understanding today. We have a joy unspeakable in our hearts. This joy that we have, the world did not give it to us, and the world could never have the power to take it away.

Just because we have Jesus in our life today does not mean that we do not go through trials and situations. It means that when we go through hard seasons, HE WILL BE WITH US. We still go through seasons. We still go through times that Jesus refines us by taking us through fire. We have seasons that are tougher than others, our life is not in any way perfect, but it is nothing like it was before. Even in the tough times, we know everything is going to be okay. We know that we have Jesus on our side and because of that we know that we can have victory in any and every situation. We don't have to live in worry or regret of the past. Instead, we choose to rejoice for our future. We get to let God use our past to show just how powerful He is. We get to allow our past to be a testimony of the glory of God!

Being filled with the Holy Ghost is something you must experience for yourself. Before I came back to Jesus, I was empty. I wasn't using but I was so ashamed of the person that I had become. Shame and condemnation are not of God. They are tools of the enemy to keep us bound, when God is trying to set us free. Even sober, I was ashamed. The anger inside of me was almost uncontrollable. The fear of relapse was incredibly loud. I was restless, discontent, and miserable. In the presence of an almighty God, chains fell, shame and guilt left, and fear bowed. What a mighty God I serve!

Slowly but surely, I began to see the chains fall off of Mike and I. That guilt, shame, and remorse turned into passion for others like us. The anger and chaos that had fueled my life for so long, turned into something God could use for His glory in prayer. I know without a shadow of a doubt that I am able to fight in prayer because I have fought my whole life. God took my aggressive nature and turned it for good. Knowing who God truly is and allowing Him to have an encounter with me was the best decision I've ever made.

We are completely free from any form of addiction that once snuffed out our hope. We are free from the shame. We are free from the guilt. Jesus broke our chains and set us free. Today, we know that the spirit of the Lord is upon us and we are anointed to bring hope. Today, I know that together, Michael and I make the enemy nervous. We know that we are called by God according to His purpose and we do not take the call on our lives lightly. What an honor it is to be called and used of God. We are chosen to share the gospel and we aren't backing down until addiction lets our people go! We are passionate for people that are just like we were. More than anything else in this whole world, we want to be soul winners. We want people to see our lives and see Jesus. We want to see others set free. There is good news for the captives, this liberty is for all who are bound. This news is for all who are broken. You too, can be made whole.

A songwriter says it like this, "amazing grace, how sweet the sound, I once was lost, but now I'm found". As my husband and I placed one foot in front of the other, grace met us every step of the way. If you are reading this and you think that you are too far gone and that there isn't a way out, that is not true. There is room for you at the foot of the cross. There is freedom with your name on it. There is life after tragedy. God has carved out a space specifically for you. If you have secretly suffered in silence, scared of what people may think about you, know that fear is a liar. If you have made yourself believe that there isn't a God that loves you, I beg you to reconsider. If nothing else I have said has resonated, please let this pierce your heart – it does not matter what you have done, Jesus forgives. It does not matter where you have been, Jesus saves. It does not matter how big your mess is, Jesus redeems. I have seen Him take the biggest messes and turn them into the biggest messages. Let Him do that for you too.

I have seen and lived in the goodness of God and I know that you can be totally free. No one can tell me He can't do it, because I know that He can. I know that you can be free from the guilt and shame that has you crippled. I know that you can be free from the anger and chaos that rules your life. I know that you can be free from the bondage of yourself. I know that you never have to use drugs again. You never have to abandon your family again. You never have to live in and out of addiction's cycle, ever again. You **DO NOT** have to live defeated and plagued by sin any longer. I know now that there **IS** a way out! His name is Jesus!

Jesus has made a way for us to be free. Salvation is free and it is for everyone who wants it. You must decide that you want it. If He did it for us, He can do it for you. I will share this solution with everyone I can, because there is freedom in the name of Jesus. The name of the Lord is a strong tower, and if you need saving, you should run into it, Proverbs 18:10. Acts 2:38, **will** set you free. It is the truth. The truth that set me free.

Acts 2:38 says, "Repent and be baptized, every one of you, in the name of Jesus Christ for the remission of your sins and you shall receive the gift of the Holy Ghost." It is clearly stated, and it is evident that it will set you free. Don't let anyone sway you from what it says. It does not say title(s), it says name! The Bible tells us that there is NO other name, given among men, whereby we MUST be saved. There is no other saving name. There is no other delivering name. There is no other blood that will do, except HIS blood and HIS name. The powerful name of Jesus. When we applied the right name to our lives, chains broke, generational curses were halted, and we get to live in complete freedom today.

I encourage you to find a church that preaches the Acts 2:38 message and that baptizes in Jesus' name! I tell people all the time, if you've tried everything else and it has all failed, try Jesus. He has never failed, and He never will. There isn't a battle that He has ever lost. Go all in and give Jesus more than you gave your addiction. Go all in and give God more than you gave your life of sin. My husband and I are living proof that if you seek Jesus with as much as you sought your next high, incredible things can happen. Don't take my word for it, try it for yourself. Get to know this truth for yourself!

We are living in a day where we need people to stand up for what is right and live their life according to the word of God. Not what society or false doctrine says but what the word of God says. We need people who will stand up for the things of God regardless of what the world and the mainstream media try to brainwash us with. We need a generation that will fight for the things of God, because eternity is at stake. We need a generation of saints who are not afraid to be laughed at and ridiculed for holding onto biblical principles. I will stand on what is right, even if I stand alone. I will live a life of biblical integrity regardless of what the world thinks of me. My husband and I will fight hell for the very souls that Jesus came and died for. If there was ever a time to stand on the truth that Jesus laid out for us, it is now. The time is now. Take a stand, right now!

I pray that this has spoken to your heart. I'm grateful that I'm able to share my testimony instead of someone sharing my memories. This could very well be an obituary filled with statements like "she was", "she did" and "she had", but it's not. Instead, it's a testament of how far God reached to restore me; to resurrect the work in which He had begun from day one. It could be a past tense account given by someone else, instead, God saw fit for me to get to tell it myself! Oh, I'm so in love with Him!

If you are not in addiction, I pray that after hearing my story, you can now see how you can help someone else that is. I pray that you can take the words on these pages and somehow apply them to whatever it is that you may be struggling with in hopes of freeing yourself, in hopes of allowing Jesus to free you too. There is someone waiting on you to love them back to life. You are the only Jesus some people will ever see. We don't have to get good to get God, we get God so that we can get good! Will you love them back to life? Will you lead them to the only truth that can set us all free? Do it for them, do it for you, do it for me. Most of all, do it for Jesus. My name is Amber and I am a ProdiGAL!

Worthlessness:

Lacking worth (equivalent in value to the sum or item specified), valueless, useless

Worthy is defined as having or showing the qualities or abilities that merit recognition in a specified way. There are so many people suffering from the feeling of being unworthy. I believe this causes so much trauma in some of our lives because it causes us to accept things we wouldn't, if we truly understood who God has called us to be from the beginning.

Whether we want to believe it or acknowledge it or not, this world is ruled by spirits. This is why we have to learn to operate in the spiritual realm. There are so many demonic forces panning for our souls. The Bible says the enemy roams the Earth seeking whom he may destroy (1 Peter 5:8). The spirit of worthlessness can snuff out the promises of God before they even begin to form. It takes hold of our mind first. The mind is a fragile space. If we allow the enemy to take hold of our thoughts then he has the advantage to get us to believe the lies he tells us.

For example, take Adam and Eve. God told them that they could eat of every tree in the garden, except one. So, you know what the enemy did? He planted seeds in Eve's mind to cause her to focus on the one tree she wasn't supposed to eat from instead of rejoicing over all the others that she could indulge in. This is how distraction will cause a detour in our destiny. The enemy will get us to form thoughts that we would never even think of and then he will get us to believe them.

This is how worthlessness comes about. It begins as a seed. Maybe that seed is someone telling us as a child that we aren't good enough, that we will never amount to anything or that we are worthless. Maybe it is the actions of an absent parent or the abuse from someone who was supposed to love and protect you with their own life. Whatever the cause, worthlessness starts with that small seed that tells us that we are unworthy of love, of recognition or of any effort at all. Once that seed is planted, I believe that we unconsciously begin to water it and allow it to grow.

We water it with acceptance. We accept the situations that happen to us and the words spoken to us in those moments because we don't know any different. We haven't been shown anything different up until that point, so why would we think we could be worthy of anything but the bare minimum. No one has ever shown us that we are top tier, worthy of respect, love and saving.

We have to make the choice to decide that we are worthy of goodness in this life. If we continue to accept what the enemy says about us, then we will never see the things of God fully come to pass in our lives. We have to be willing to stand up as the victors we are and take the dominion and authority He granted to us. We are children of the King of kings and the Lord of lords! A royal priesthood (1 Peter 2:9); how dare we live our lives as peasants!

God said that we are worthy of love. He said that we are worthy of life. He said that we are worthy of time. How? On Calvary, thousands of years ago, He sacrificed His own life in hopes of us having a chance to live out our own. He bled for us. He died for us. He rose for us. So that we might get a chance at life filled with abundance far beyond what we could ever comprehend.

1 Corinthians 6:20 AMP You were bought with a price (you were actually purchased with the precious blood of Jesus and made His own). So then, honor and glorify God with your body.

Isaiah 43:4 AMP Because you are precious in My sight, You are honored and I love you, I will give other men in return for you and other peoples in exchange for your life.

Jeremiah 29:11 AMP For I know the plans and thoughts that I have for you, says the Lord, plans for peace and well-being and not for disaster, to give you a future and a hope.

Psalms 139:14 AMP I will give thanks and praise to You, for I am fearfully and wonderfully made; Wonderful are Your works, and my soul knows it very well.

Romans 8:32 AMP He who did not spare (even) His own Son, but gave Him up for us all, how will He not also, along with Him, graciously give us all things?

Gina Johnson is a 40-year-old, god-fearing, single mother of three beautiful young ladies (RaShay, LaParis & LeeOma). She is heavily involved at her home church Greater Faith Louisville Central and also connected to many organizations in the city. Gina loves people. When asking others about how they would describe her, there was a consensus in the words powerful, encouraging and inspiring. She was a lifelong resident of Louisville, KY until recently when she purchased a new home and moved to Indiana. Her favorite past times are time spent with her grands (Cameron, Rah'Leah and Ry'Lee), writing new literature and trying new restaurants. If she is in the room, you can count on there also being laughter and some sort of empowerment happening there. She is a poet who has poems installed in different areas of the city and she published her first book of poetry earlier this year. "When Prayer and Poetry Collide," can be found on Amazon. She travels the city performing poetry at different events and is working on publishing more books in the near future.

Her testimony is a powerful one, like many others, including the others from the ladies in this book. She shares with us in great detail, the story of victim to victor, conquered to conqueror and chump to champ! She may stumble, maybe even fall, but what you can always count on with her, is that she will always get back up.

One of her favorite things to say is, "I am not a thermometer, I am a thermostat. The temperature of the room is set by me."

Her favorite scripture right now is none other than Jeremiah 29:11 NIV "For I know the plans I have for you," declares the Lord, "plans to prosper you and not to harm you, plans to give you hope and a future." For far too long she lived her life on her terms, it's high time she gave God His turn.

Lost & Found

Have you ever felt as if you were walking dead? As if you simply didn't have the lung capacity to take another single breath. Like your next breath was so far away that you couldn't reach it. There was no way you were going to be able to obtain what you needed to, in order to breathe. Has your body ever been so weighted down that you felt as if you couldn't take another step or that your legs were too heavy for you to even lift? You couldn't even begin to mimic the motion of right, left, one foot in front of the other. Has your mind played so many tricks on you that you were unable to fathom getting up? Have you ever been in such a place that rock bottom seemed to be the place where you belonged; where you were destined to dwell forever? There was nothing more for you, nothing greater for you to come in your future. Have you ever been to that place? Stuck in a place of desolation forever. I know I'm not the only one because the enemy fights us all. Unfortunately, sometimes he uses our own being to fight against us.

He uses our mind, he uses our tongues, he uses our limbs to make choices, each and every day, that threaten our salvation. These choices kill us spiritually, even though, we are still here in the physical form. We succumb to those threats in our minds first. So, we become the enemy to our own being because we believe the ridiculous falsehoods that he feeds to us.

It's amazing how easily we will quit. I know some will say, well it wasn't easy, that was a long time coming. That was years of abuse, years of trauma, years of disappointment after disappointment, years of godlessness that mounted up and bubbled over. It overflowed and I was just done. I let it. However, as mothers, we tend to never give up the fight when it comes to our children. When it comes to those around us whom we love dearly, our mothers, fathers, siblings and grandparents, we will stand toe-to-toe and let the devil know, I wish you would! But, let it be about us. Let it be about ourselves and things for us and we will easily believe that we don't deserve the same fight, the same gumption or the same drive. We tend to easily forfeit, when the fight is about ourselves. Nobody better not ever mess with our loved ones, we will never give up the fight for them but for some odd, strange reason, we tend to bow out when the enemy comes for us.

Humph, well, this here is my ProdiGAL moment. This is my testimony. This is my story. The story about the time I chose to GET UP!

I remember laying in spiritual vomit. It's the only way I can describe what was happening to me. It's the only plausible verbiage to describe the mess that I had made for myself to lay in. I lay on the bed in the posture of someone who had been hung over from the night before and I, myself, had never been drunk. I had never consumed alcohol at a level that made me ill the next day or while intaking it. It was never my thing. I had barely even tried alcohol before. However, I knew what this posture looked like because I had seen it on others close to me before and in the movies. My head was positioned at an angle to where it was almost hanging off of the bed, but it was still on the pillow. My right leg was bent at the knee and my toes were peeking out from under the comforter a bit. My right arm was fully exposed, dangling over the edge of the bed, almost coming in contact with the floor. I was laying there for I don't even remember how long, staring blankly at the wall. A single tear escaped my eye and cascaded down my cheek. I didn't try to stop it. I didn't try to swat it away. I let it roll onto the pillowcase and saturate it with its saltiness. Then another escaped, and another and another.

I was in such emotional pain. I don't think any physical pain that I had endured in my life could amount to this. It couldn't hold a candle to the way my heart was shattered in that moment. Not even childbirth measured up to the debilitating agony I was experiencing. Not even umbilical hernia repair surgeries, in which I went through, back-to-back. Not even the partial hysterectomy I was forced to have, due to fibroids the size of grapefruits ruining my life, or so it felt like anyway. Let me be extra people, ha. This pain that I was experiencing, I had never experienced before. I could feel nothing, I could hear nothing, in that moment. The space that I was in was foreign to me. I had no idea how I had even gotten there. Well, in that moment, I didn't. However, as I continued to grow and become who I was supposed to be in God in the first place, I can look back on that and see that I do know how I got there now. It was a lack of hope. My life had become an endless cycle of prayerlessness. I was completely destitute of hope, weary and downtrodden because I was tired of disappointment. I was tired of thinking that things would be different, that things would or could change and then they didn't. I was tired of feeling as if my prayers didn't work. They were the only ones God never received. Like God, somehow, had put my prayers, specifically, on mute. He gladly received everyone else's though. Like I had been blocked from Him and He was unable to receive my messages as if I was communicating with the God of the universe through Messenger. Crazy right?

I had believed for so many things and there was so much stuff that had been spoken that I believed for that had yet to come to pass then and I didn't feel as if they ever would. I was just so tired of the waiting room. You know?

I know we go to the doctor and baby, none of us are okay with the waiting room. None of us want to be there. That's why we make appointments right? The waiting room is always filled with different backgrounds, different social and financial statuses, different experiences and sometimes we don't understand those things when we are sitting in the same space with them. Sometimes we look around a waiting room and simply don't understand why we are even there and all we want is to get out of there. Fortunately for us, the waiting room actually becomes a place where we are prepared for our appointment. It is in the waiting room that we sit, and wait. I know that sounds so elementary, but that's what we do. We sit and we wait our turn to be called. We feel as if it will take forever and it will never be our turn, but the reality is, eventually, it will be our turn. However, none of us want to hurry up and wait. If we do though, at the appointed time, we are called. That's the way God works right? He calls us for appointed times, but none of us like to wait to be called, we just want the appointment. We have to understand though, that the appointment will never come without the waiting period, without the waiting room.

Back to my story. As I lay there, eventually, many thoughts began to race in my mind. Many thoughts came to me and I begin to think, what am I doing? How did I get here? Why has this happened to me? I remember calling out to God, saying to Him, please don't sift me. Please don't let me go. I'm in a wilderness right now that I am unfamiliar with and I, me, the victor, the conqueror, the giant killer; I have no idea how to fight. I have lost my ability to win the victory. I have lost the energy to lift my head and I am on the verge of drowning in this storm. Humph. Whew, writing this brings it back so freshly in my mind and tears are gathering on the brims of my eyelids, this time filled with gratefulness to God because He heard my plea. I wasn't on mute. He wasn't blocking my prayers; He was actually gathering them up waiting for the perfect time to execute His response. He heard me when I thought I was in a forest with tall trees that muffled my sound. He heard me when I thought I was in a desert place that stretched miles and miles without any sign of life. He heard me. Speaking about those things had been such a burden, such a heaviness, such a painful experience to come to the realization of. However, it was in that very moment when I gave up, when I realized that I had been walking dead, that God stepped in.

It wasn't that I didn't know it while I was in that mess, because I did. I just decided to allow my life to play out on autopilot in that season. I hit cruise control and just went with it. Living for God is not like that. We cannot expect great things living on cruise control. We have to be cognizant to what is happening around us and be mindful of our actions. The saddest thing about living like that is that we be knowing that we are dead wrong and we will continue to be dead wrong instead of fixing it. Usually, we have become too prideful or too shameful to correct our wrongs. Just like flesh, isn't it? I tell you. I think that we somehow unconsciously, well sometimes, continue down the wrong path because we don't want to exert the energy needed to turn around and correct our wrong turn. So, we just stay the course, knowing it's going to lead us to a dead end. My, my, my. It was in the moment that I gave up my will that He was able to move and allow me to experience His will instead.

So, I feel like I am kind of painting this picture for you backwards. That's alright, because there is no back of the book for you to read and see that I won. So, I let the cat out of the bag in the beginning to show you that God won! He always will!

Anyhow, I had such a terrible bout with low self-esteem for majority of my life. As a young, heavy-set girl, I never equated me and beauty as an item. The two just didn't go together. I was always one of the smartest people I knew. I could put some words together in a heartbeat and I could love the unloved and I could cause others to smile when they really wanted to frown, however, I didn't know how to do those things for myself. I didn't know what it meant to love me and the older I got the more I realized that had to do with the lack of a father figure in my life. Young ladies truly depend on fathers for validation, safety, security and love. I never felt as if I had those things.

I did have an uncle that tried his very best to treat me as his own. He always picked me up, took me to church, gave me gifts and shared his wife and children with me anytime I wanted to be a plus one with them, he would allow me and my sister to come if she wanted to. He was/is definitely Uncle-Dad. It was always a blessing to have that relationship, however, he wasn't my father. He wasn't around daily.

At a young age, I learned to equate beauty with what others thought of me. How others treated me, was how worthy I thought I was. Big-boned wasn't part of the equation of beauty. Larger lips and foreheads weren't apart of the equation. Wider hips and thick short hair were not part of that equation either. I simply didn't love me, for a very long time. If I didn't love me, how could anyone else? Especially, God. I had such a terrible sense of unworthiness. I didn't feel worthy of love, other people's time or visibility period. I felt unseen, completely invisible, unheard, and unappreciated most of my life. It morphed into this beast as an adult, really in my early teen years, where I accepted pretty much anything from anyone. Mainly men. How could I deserve respect or demand anyone to treat me like anything when I didn't feel worthy of it to begin with?

I have only had 2 serious relationships in my entire life. Both birthed children out of wedlock that I was forced to tend to without their fathers at some point. I have always had a great support system in my mom. She was then and is still always willing to help me in any way she can. I remember when I had my first daughter in high school and I would cry in the middle of the night because I would be so exhausted because that child just would not go to sleep. She literally didn't sleep through a whole night until she was about 3 years old. My mom was a trooper though. She would come into my room and take her and tell me to rest for school.

"I simply didn't love me, for a very long time. If I didn't love me, how could anyone else? Especially, God."

She was a working single mother herself. She still had me and my younger sister in the house, but that didn't stop her from trying to make my life easier, even when I had made the wrong choice at the time. She didn't disown me for becoming a teenage mother. She didn't berate me for it. She always helped me. She always made sure I was taken care of and still tries to do this now and I'm 40. She would take my daughter to her room with her and try to calm her and get her to sleep. She would also get up in the morning and get her ready and take her with her to work. She worked at a daycare and my daughter went to the daycare she worked at. I would get up and get ready for school and go get on the bus. My mom has always been such a great blessing to my life. I'm more than grateful for the blessing she has always been to me.

So, the first serious relationship birthed 2 children and the last, whom I married, birthed 1. All girls. Lucky me, right? I would have more girls to pass down this inflicted generational curse to as if it was a prized possession. As if it was something valuable, they could cherish like a family heirloom worth millions of dollars that could one day bail them out of bankruptcy. No, not lucky me. I would make many mistakes while trying to do my best to give them their best chance at having the greatest quality of life I could offer them. It wasn't until later in life, when I became an adult, that I realized that some of this happened due to me growing up fatherless. There was never anyone to show me that I had value, so, I tried to find value wherever I could. Unfortunately, I would fail them over and over because I was ill-equipped to really understand what I needed to give them as a mother at such a young age.

This young girl, who was born, raised and dwelled in many Louisville housing projects, wasn't worthy of much value. You could only imagine the types of things I experienced, witnessed and endured in this type of environment. A poverty mindset is a beast. It will bring so much havoc to your life. I have found that people with this type of mindset are content with crumbs and don't have any desire to ever "bake their own cake". Handouts are enough for them. Barely getting by is enough for them because they are content in a place of mediocrity.

Poverty is the devil's poison. I say this because it is not just in finances that people remain impoverished. It begins as a mindset. People settle into contentment and don't try to become anything more then what they've always known their lineage to be. You have a select few that may go above and beyond and look for better things for themselves, but the majority will decide to be the same. I saw this so many times, even within myself, growing up in the projects. It was exciting to live this way. It was fun and normal. So why would I want anything other than my norm? We were never created to be seen begging bread, so we should never settle for the bottom. However, the bottom is the best launching pad to break barriers from. At the bottom, you know that you can't go anywhere but up.

Now, don't get me wrong. Living in the communities I lived in as a child wasn't all bad. It was actually more positive than negative, but the negative was definitely present. People on the outside looking in or listening to everything the media had to say, wouldn't understand the dynamics of that type of neighborhood. In the 80's and 90's, it wasn't as bad as you would see now. It was a village. People looked out for one another there. There was crime, but there was love too.

However, it was a breeding ground for poverty. The mentality of some people living there was to not want any more from life than what they saw there. As I said before, it was the norm. I remember myself as a teenager being excited that I was getting closer to 18 so that I could get my own apartment in the projects (Southwick specifically). I wasn't excited about college, about entrepreneurism or homeownership. Let me say this. I had at one point been excited about having a different life. However, becoming a teenage mom rerouted my plans. I had received a full ride scholarship to a great school out of state. I had always been a scholar in school so this was the greatest achievement of my life thus far. I was devastated when I found out that I had strangled my chance at a different life with my own two hands and took away my chances at having that life with the choice I made, one time.

I'm grateful for my daughter though, so don't get it twisted. I made that choice. She didn't. God doesn't make mistakes, people do, but God does not. This little girl would become a lifesaver for me. For a young girl who didn't fully understand the concept of love, I would be gifted an unconditional love in her. She saved my life when it was dark and cloudy. She gave my life meaning and value at 15, when I never thought it had any. She gave me reason to keep pushing every day and making a better way for her, as best I could. She didn't sleep through the night until she was about three years old, but she was the light of so many lives. She was a ball of energy and constantly kept everyone laughing. She still does, to this day. If she is in the room, you know that laughter will happen there.

Anyways, I was excited to one day live the same way I had always lived. While it was unsafe to others, it was a safe place to me, because it was what I had always known. The enemy works in this same manner. If he can get us stagnant, comfortable and content, then he can get us to turn away from God. If we don't want any more out of life or from God than what He has already blessed us with, then we aren't a huge threat for the enemy. However, when we choose to step into our callings and accept what is going to be required of us, then the enemy knows that he has a fight on his hands. A poverty mindset is not of God. God is a god of prosperity. He wants us to have life and not mediocrely, but abundantly (John 10:10 KJV). We cannot grow into the deep things of God, nor the true blessings of God with a poverty-stricken mindset.

So, eventually I did turn 18 and I did get that project apartment that I was dreaming of as a teen, in a different housing project though because the one I wanted had been demolished and rebuilt as "affordable housing". When I moved into my apartment, I allowed my daughter's father to live there also. I am clueless to what truth is in this moment. I knew the meaning of a few words, Christian, sin, pastor, church, but I didn't have any revelation of living for God being anything more than church attendance.

My house, like my mother's when I was young, was the cool house. It was where everybody came to have fun. You could daily find us on the porch, blasting ungodly music, playing cards while those who partook in things such as drinking and smoking did their thing. I was never into any of that, but I hung around lots of people who were. You could find us having rap sessions in my yard. I knew quite a few of the local artists and some of them would sometimes stop by and we would spit some bars together here and there. I began writing and rapping then. I enjoyed it. It was something to do to pass the time. I was so unhappy with my life, writing and rapping at least gave me a place where I could talk about life without anybody knowing it was about me personally or having anyone judging because rap was just rap. I could say whatever I wanted to say, even the things I was afraid to say to the people who had hurt me or disrespected me, I could easily put it in a song. It was a form of therapy for me. Later, poetry would do the same. They are really one and the same, in my opinion.

Back then, I didn't understand the importance of living a godly life. I had heard some sermons that spoke about Jesus' return and not to sin, but they never pricked my heart. So, I lived my life in fornication, rebellion and sin. In the process, I birthed my second child. I have never known anyone to have a baby as good as her. She was the most beautiful baby. Always smiling and giggling at the small chance that she would be awake. She literally slept majority of her infant life. On many occasions, I had to wake her up to feed her, bathe her and change her. She would just be sleep. So content and peaceful. She still is like that now. She would much rather be in her bed or at home than anywhere else. She is one of the biggest introverts I've ever known. Her and my youngest daughter. The oldest, not so much. She is the extrovert of all extroverts. My middle daughter is the most affectionate though I believe. She would be the one to come and hug my neck and tell me she loved me before the others. She didn't mind letting me know that I was cherished.

As I was saying, I never fully comprehended what living for God was back then. However, I know now that the word says for us to get in the book for ourselves (2 Timothy 2:15 KJV). The truth was out there, I just had no desire to seek it out at that time. I wasn't giving tithes or offerings; I wasn't praying before making decisions and I wasn't asking or allowing God to be the head of my life. I wasn't a bad person in my book, not then and not now. However, I was so lost and didn't even know it. I had no idea what the apostle's doctrine was. Even in my spiritual blindness, God was preparing a place for me in His kingdom. How great is He? That even though I never made an effort to know Him, He still made sure that there would be a way of escape for me. He still made sure that I would, one day, get to know Him.

That's the type of God that I serve. He is a gentleman. He is patient, forgiving, loving and kind. Even when I had no desire to choose Him, He still chose me. He never saw me the way that I saw myself. I was not this broken, fatherless, weary, worthless, and hopeless being. No, He saw beauty where I saw ashes. He saw potential, where I only saw and felt pain. He saw a victor when I wanted so badly to remain a victim. A victim of circumstance, a victim of self-inflicted wounds and a victim of ignorance. He refused to allow me to become the things that the enemy wanted me so badly to believe I was and always would be. Instead, He shielded me from that mentality.

"Even when I had no desire to choose Him, He still chose me. He never saw me the way that I saw myself. I was not this broken, fatherless, weary, worthless and hopeless being. No, He saw beauty, where I saw ashes."

Slowly, He planted good thoughts in my mind about who I was and who I would become. Slowly, He changed me from unbeliever, to believer. I can never repay Him for what He has done for me. When He chose me, He chose my family members also. When He chose me, He chose my friends, my coworkers, the person at the pump next to me, the people connected to me on social media and anyone else I come in contact with, because when they have seen me, they have seen my Father. I wear His glory on me every day in hopes that people can see Him in me and it would become so magnetic that they are drawn unto Him whenever they are near me. I want His love and light to shine bright to all the world around me so that others know that, such as I have, they can have also.

Fast forward a little bit again. Now, I have moved out of this housing project. I have two children and I am living in the west end of Louisville now. I am with my future husband living in a two-bedroom apartment, working two jobs, and trying to raise my kids the best way I know how. I still have yet to have an encounter with God that would change my life. I would visit my cousins church seldomly, but for the most part, I had no relationship or connection to God. Daily, I would routinely go about my life. Sometimes I would sit and think how different my life might have been if I had of went off to college on that scholarship I had earned back in high school. I had always wanted to go to college and get a degree and be the first of my mothers' children to do so. So, I enrolled in school. My home life was too hectic though, so, that didn't last long at all.

Over the course of several years, we would move several times. One time included my children and I moving into a transitional housing facility. I became pregnant a third time and would actually deliver my baby while living here. While living at this facility, I had begun to go to church with my sister. I always looked up to my eldest sister as a kid because she seemed to be so put together. Even though we came from where we came from, she carried herself differently. She worked, took great care of her kids, went to school and tried to make a better way for herself and them.

I remember finding out I was pregnant with my youngest daughter. I was so scared. I had already felt like I was failing at parenting with the first two. I remember calling my sister and wailing on the phone to the point it scared her. She didn't know what was going on and she couldn't make out my incoherent babbling. I'm laughing thinking of the sight of this now. I know she wanted to slap me when she realized what I was saying. Ha. I remember her saying, "what, slow down, what are you saying, I can't understand you". Then when I got myself together enough to talk clearly where she could understand she said, "girl I'm going to kill you, I thought something tragic had happened". The nerve of her, this was tragic for me. How would I be able to take care of another baby when I was already struggling taking care of the other two? She calmed me down. She prayed with me over the phone and assured me that everything would be alright. After hanging up with her, I laid down and slept the most peaceful sleep. God is just so amazing like that. He will give you rest, in the midst of chaos, if you ask Him.

My sister began to attend church with one of my cousins. It was an apostolic church. The transitional housing center that I lived in was within minutes of the church she was attending. I had attended this church as a visitor many times before. It had actually moved twice before being at the location near the transitional housing center. I remember being in labor with my daughter throughout the entire day that Sunday. But I had begun to fall in love with "church", notice I said church and not God, so I didn't want to miss it. I had a serious case of FOMO (fear of missing out) when it came to a church service. I simply wanted to be there. I wanted a change for my life and for the lives of my children. I had already felt like such a failure in not providing a stable place for them to live, not living my life according to God's word and wedding before pregnancy so that they weren't born out of wedlock and not seeking to know more about God sooner. So, church became another notch in the schedule of my routine.

I ended up getting a really nice job, making good money for that time. I moved into a really nice apartment in old Louisville, bigger than some people's houses. My mom was always at my house, helping me with my kids, cooking, cleaning, doing whatever she could to make my life easier as usual. My cousin even came and stayed with me there for a little while. That apartment was huge. I also got to live near Uncle Thomas. He was my future husband's uncle. One of the kindest spirits you ever did meet. He was always trying to help us with things. My middle daughter absolutely loved him. He nicknamed her "Oatmeal" because every time she would visit him, they would eat oatmeal together.

While living here, my future husband would also get his own apartment as well. It was in another housing project. A different one than the one's I had already lived in before. He wanted to have his own space. We weren't married, so that made complete sense that he would. Also, I had been going to church regularly now so I had been thinking about all the things I had done incorrectly. Thinking about how God must feel to know that I was living with a man who wasn't my husband, fornicating and rebelling against what I was reading in His word. I believe I had even one day told him that I wouldn't sleep with him anymore, that he had to live right and go to church and all that stuff. So, one day, he came in and proposed.

I was still the same broken little girl inside, even though I was an adult. I was still carrying so many of the burdens of my past. I remember thinking, oh wow, me? Somebody wants to marry me? How lucky am I that anyone would ask me? I was ashamed that I wasn't giving my kids the life I felt they deserved and I was ashamed of not being further along in life because I had so many dreams and aspirations when I was younger and it seemed as if my life was passing me by. So, what other answer could I give except yes? I may never get the chance again to be somebody's wife. That sounded good to me. I would get to tell people that I, me, this broken little girl, had a husband. He wobbled down to one knee, I'm sure he was out of his body. I wasn't even sure he knew what he was doing. I was thinking he would wake up and not even remember that he had done this. However, he didn't. He woke up excited about it and thanking me for saying yes. I thought, this must be the right choice. Marrying him would fix the issue of fornication. So, of course, this must be the right choice.

I went to work and showed off my little ring. I was so happy, or so it seemed then. However, soon I would come to the realization that I wasn't happy at all. That I was still missing a piece to my puzzle. Maybe this marriage would be that missing link. I wasn't sure, but now that I had said yes and had gotten gifts from the people at work and all of that, I couldn't go back. I couldn't change my mind or say that I was having second thoughts or that I was scared out of my mind that it wouldn't work. I hated failing. I wasn't really a perfectionist, but I didn't like to fail. I'm sure no one does. I remember making a terrible deal with God. I told Him, "God, you know that I have always said that I just don't want to be alone. I will deal with anything if it means I won't be alone. I have been suffocated by the spirit of loneliness all of my life. I have always felt invisible. If you will allow me to do this, I will do whatever I can to make it work. If it doesn't, then I will just have to be alone for the rest of my life. But I know that it will work because You don't want us to fornicate and if I marry Him, I won't be committing any sins anymore. "

It was the response of someone who was on spiritual formula. I was still drinking infant milk. I hadn't even graduated to the gallon jug yet. How could I think I could negotiate my fate with the God of the universe? It was such an elementary prayer. I think about that now and it was such a selfish prayer. All I talked about was what I wanted; what I thought I needed. I never asked God to help me decide. I never asked God what He wanted for my life and if it was the right decision. I thought I knew more than God. I told God; this is what I'm doing. That is never the way we should operate. I am so thankful that I have learned to put Him at the front of my decision-making, not at the end. I am so grateful that I have learned to involve Him, 100%, in things concerning me, my children and now grandchildren. I no longer have any desire to tell God what is best for me because He knows what is best for me. I surrender all to Him.

I am pretty sure I wasn't the first or the last to get cold feet or have second thoughts about marrying someone. It is such a huge decision to make. It is one of the biggest decisions we will make in our lives. It's actually probably the most important decision. This is your person. You are making the choice to spend the rest of your life with this person because divorce was never supposed to be an option. It was never meant to be a part of the equation. So, I stood there in my living room, with a justice of the peace, my mom, my cousin and my soon-to-be husband and I was scared out of my mind. I never claimed to know God in a way that I heard Him. That I could hear His instructions, but I felt something so strong in my spirit telling me not to do it that day, but it was too late. I couldn't go back. I had paid this man to marry us, I had gotten the marriage license, I had given my soon-to-be husband my yes. I had no choice but to go through with it now. If I didn't, how would everyone look at me? Would they think I was a fraud or a fake? Would they not take me seriously in other decisions that I made in the future? Would he leave me for not sticking to my word? How would he feel if I rejected him now? I couldn't do that. It was too late. I was committed to I do.

Looking back, I totally understand why I was having those feelings standing there that day. God deals in perfect timing and perfecting of people. That does not mean that He makes any of us perfect, because nobody is perfect. However, it does mean that He equips us for every season of our lives. We weren't equipped for that season yet. The timing was not right. I was not spiritually mature enough to be marrying anyone, neither was he. I was not prepared to be anyone's wife; he wasn't prepared to be a husband. I was not living a holy life myself and neither was he. Neither of us were prepared to become one. We were unequally yoked. Neither of us really knew anything about living for God. Neither of us had searched the scripture for ourselves in a way that would have brought us true revelation of what we should have done. I don't even recall a time that we had ever even prayed together, nevertheless read the Bible together. All I knew was I didn't want the sin of fornication hanging over me anymore and marriage would remedy that. That alone was worth it to me. Oh, how wrong I would be.

I was trying to solve sin problems with quick fixes and like many other things, there is a process. There is a waiting period, as I spoke of before. I was ill-equipped for the wait. God knew that He had so much in store for me and He knew what I needed to be equipped with. He knew that my lack of preparation would only cause me and others harm. I wish I could do things differently. If I could go back in time, I would make different choices to ensure that there weren't so many casualties from my choices. I would give up my plans for God's. God's plan for our lives is not to cause us harm, but to make us grow. He only wants us to prosper (Jeremiah 29:11 KJV). Since I can't, I choose to live for Him now. Allow His direction to lead me down the paths He wants me to travel and let Him order my steps. He is the author and finisher of my faith. No one knows better than He. I put complete trust in Him, to cover me, to protect me and to mold me into what He wants me to be for His glory.

Soon, we moved again. This time we were moving into my husband's apartment because I had lost my job and could no longer afford the nice apartment I had in Old Louisville. I owed the housing authority from the last time I had lived there because I left without paying the last months' rent and I had to pay that in order to be added to his lease. So, I made the payment and they moved us into a two-bedroom apartment instead. We lived there for a little while and then they decided that they would demolish those as well so we would all be moving again. I was so excited because we were going to get to move into a house possibly because of the demolition, we were given the option of receiving Section 8. Well, come to find out we didn't qualify because of something on his record. So, we yet again had to move into another housing project apartment. I was moving back to where I had gotten my first apartment this time.

I was so angry, hurt, and sad about this. I didn't want to live in the projects anymore. I wanted something different, something better. I was tired of it. I was finally waking up from the slumber of mediocrity and I was ready for elevation. I had started going to school right before we moved this time. I wanted to try to finish what I had started before, but again, life happened and that didn't happen that time either. I can't even describe to you all how upset I was about this last transition. I couldn't believe that we had the opportunity to choose a better neighborhood for the kids, but before we could even get it, it was snatched away. I really had to deal with that disappointment. It really did a number on me mentally. I did not want to move back downtown. He didn't either, but we had no choice.

So, we move yet again. I decided that I was not going to continue this cycle. Our relationship was struggling tremendously with all the transitions and life happening to us. We were becoming more and more distant from one another and I was reminding myself that I had told God that I would withstand anything the day I said I do. I had to deal with the consequences of my choices, no matter what they would be, because I owed God. We were constantly arguing and at odds. I was so functionally depressed it isn't even funny. I was living my life on autopilot. There were days I didn't want to get up, but I had to because I had to take care of my kids. There were days, months, years even where I didn't even care about myself. I didn't care how I looked, I didn't care how I dressed, I didn't care about cleanliness or anything. All I knew was, I was still missing something. I was still broken. Unfortunately for me, in this season, I didn't have the energy to pursue it anymore. I was just going to live my life on autopilot, hoping that one day, something would eventually change.

Over the course of several years, he had suffered some great losses. He lost his grandmother, his mother, his biological father, his best friend, his best friend's mother and sister, other close friends, cousins, his favorite aunt and uncles; so many people. Over a span of 10 years, he had been burdened by tremendous grief and I had no idea how to help him. So, to add to our already strained relationship, we had grief, depression, and disappointment after disappointment to bare. It was so heavy. Our home was so heavy. There was no peace there. There was no joy there, because there was no God there. I didn't really understand it then. However, I definitely understand it now. I wish I would have known then what I know now. I would have run to the arms of God so much sooner to alleviate some of the deep despair that we experienced together.

One day, my children made the choice to want to go to church. There had been flyers placed on our door week after week. I would remove them, read them, and then trash them. I was going to church sporadically because my vehicle would break down and then no one would pick me up so if I didn't have transportation I just didn't go. I began walking my children over to the elementary school gymnasium every Sunday for church. I would take them and then come back and pick them up. They would come home excited about what they had learned and anxious to return.

One day, I decided, I wanted some of that excitement. I wanted to feel the joy they were feeling, so I went. What did I have to lose? My life seemed to be in shambles, so it clearly couldn't get much worse than it was. Church had to be a step up from the blindness I was walking in daily. I walked into the gymnasium and I sat on the very last row in the very last seat in the room. I sat there patiently waiting for service to start and when it did, I realized the preacher was Caucasian. I immediately wanted to leave. In my head, all white preachers sounded like Ben Stein from those clear eyes commercial that used to play all the time when I was younger. I was not about to sit here and listen to that kind of preaching. There was no way I was staying there. I just needed to wait for the right moment to pass, in order to get up and walk out without being noticed.

I don't have a racist bone in my body. I love everybody. Anybody that knows me, knows that. So, I hope. However, this was too unorthodox for me to handle. I wasn't ready for that at all. I sat there plotting my exit when he began to speak. I immediately piped up and listened. The feeling of flight left me so quickly. I was intrigued by his delivery. There was a passion burning in him that said that he knew something that I didn't, but I needed to know. I immediately wanted to know! He preached his guts out that day. I caught myself rocking my leg, wanting to shout amen and stand and clap but that wasn't me. I wasn't into embarrassing myself in front of people acting or looking no fool. But I'm telling you all, something in me really wanted to. It was as if God knew I would be there. God knew what to download into his spirit to release into that gymnasium to grab my attention like never before. It worked; God had my attention that day.

I was so surprised by his preaching style that I don't even remember what he was preaching. All I knew was that I wanted to experience more. I left that service that day, determined to return the next Sunday. I couldn't believe that a Caucasian person could preach like that. I never saw that on tv. Whenever I saw a Caucasian preacher on tv, they were boring. No offense, but that was my initial assumption. I assumed that he would be no different. When I tell you all how wrong I was, take my word for it because it was far from boring.

I have since come to realize that "color" is no match for anointing. God doesn't care about the color of any of our skin. He cares about our character, our integrity and our willingness to serve Him and be used by Him. This man was not the same as any other preacher whose voice I have sat under the sound of. He was so passionate about what he was delivering. There was no doubt that He believed everything he preached and you could tell that he lived it. I gathered all of this from just one sermon. That is how life-changing this one service was for me.

There was a girl on the praise team who was also Caucasian, but she sang like she had soul. My oldest daughter would dub her "the voice" ha. She sang with such anointing and authority. She gave life to every word in every song. I was mesmerized by this place. I had to come back. So, I did. I had found a little patch of heaven in an elementary school gymnasium and I wasn't going to just leave this place without being present in it.

I began to come back, listen and retain the teachings from the pulpit. I began to desire to have my own relationship with God. A true relationship; none like I had ever had before. This was new. I began to not just rock my legs, but clap my hands, stand and shout hallelujahs to Jesus in the middle of the service. I had lost any care about what others might think of how I praised God. He deserved to be praised because of who He was and for all that He had done for me. I remember one day, Bishop (he wasn't Bishop yet then, but he is Bishop now so I have to pay honor to him), was preaching and it was like fire shut up in my soul. I was rocking my right leg so hard, no wonder it didn't detach and hop across that gymnasium on its own. Something had gotten ahold of me. I remember him saying, let it go. Out of the blue, I couldn't resist anymore. Breakthrough, broke me free of all those years of bondage and chains. I was dancing and shouting and crying and thanking God for what He was doing in my life. It was so freeing. There was a peace and a joy that came with being released from all of that heaviness from my past. I can't even truly put into words what I felt in that moment. Freedom, liberty and love. For the first time in my life, I felt worthy. I was valuable to God.

"I had to get rid of the spirit of fear in order to allow God to give me His spirit. For the spirit of God and the spirit of fear cannot abide together on the inside. One of them has to go. I chose fear."

I didn't speak in tongues that day. I felt liberty though. I remember when I did though, years later. I'm sure nobody realized that it took me years to receive the Holy Ghost. I had to get rid of the spirit of fear in order to allow God to bless me with His spirit. For the spirit of God and the spirit of fear, cannot abide together on the inside. One of them has to go. I chose fear. I was so afraid of failing that I didn't really seek it much. I think people believed I already had the Holy Ghost because I became such a worshipper. The fear of failure kept me from it for far longer than it should have.

One night, I had gone to a night service at the mother congregation in Indiana. I was sitting in the back to right of the sanctuary, praying by myself. I began to worship God and praise Him and suddenly, right there by myself He filled me with His spirit. I begin to speak in a language that was foreign to me. I had been coming to church for years by then. I was always afraid of pushing myself to that point because I felt like once that happened, I was bound to live for God. Once I had the Holy Ghost, I could never make another mistake, I could never do anything else wrong. So, as I said before, I didn't even try to seek for it. I was always a worshipper from that moment forth in the gymnasium. So, I think people assumed I had it, but I didn't. I believed I had to become "perfect" in order to receive the Holy Ghost. This is false though. The Holy Ghost does not work like that. It does help us live right; however, it won't keep us from completely making mistakes. We will not become perfect; we will make mistakes and have to correct those mistakes, even with the Holy Ghost. I learned that it wouldn't make me perfect and the altar would welcome my repentance as long as it was sincere and I turned away from sin and old ways. Repentance is not simply an apology; it is a turn around. It is a new chance to become a new creature from that moment forth.

I was so glad that I had finally yielded my spirit to God. I had been baptized at the church I went to before this with my sister while pregnant with my youngest daughter. Many times, I had the thought of being baptized again. I never acted on it but I did have the thought. Now that I am writing this, I think I will. The thought is fresh in my mind again. I know we only need to be baptized once, even if we mess up, we can just repent and turn away. However, it must be the right way, in Jesus' name. Not in titles, but in His name. The power comes from His name. That is fresh on my heart again as I type these words, so I think I'll go ahead and do it. What could it harm? My mom has recently gotten baptized at my church again also, and she too was baptized at the other church. It has given her such a fresh faith.

I know my writing is a bit different. Sorry about that, ha. If I have a thought, I have to share it. I can't help it. So, fast-forward and I have been living for God for some years now. I have tried so many times to get my husband to make the change as well. I had been bringing his clothes to church with me, anointing his clothes that were in the closet, putting oil on the tags of his t-shirts and the tongues of his shoes, covering him in prayer. I wanted God to make our family whole. However, I didn't understand that in order for God to move in any of our lives, we have to be willing to let Him. We have to be willing to receive Him, He would not force Himself on anyone but He would always extend an invitation to us. If we are not willing to be a recipient of His grace, mercy and love, then there is nothing that He can do because He gives us our own will. He gives us the choice to decide if we want to exchange that will for His.

One day a couple from church was teaching me a Bible study and he comes downstairs and joins in the Bible study with us, out of the blue. I was elated. I was so excited thinking, this is it. He is ready to leave the world alone and live for God. Nope, it didn't happen. Then one day we were at home and he came in and was discombobulated and asked for me to call people from church, he wanted to go to the church and pray. I did and we did. He prayed, we prayed, God moved. But this still wasn't the breakthrough I wanted so badly for him, for us. Our marriage needed it so deeply. The divide between us kept growing. I kept going to church and trying to live a godly life. He kept living in the street. How can two walk together, except they agree (Amos 3:3 KJV)?

We moved, again. Are you surprised? Ha. I enrolled in school, this time, I would finish. This time I would get many awards, graduate Cum Laude and even have the honor of giving the graduation speech. I was so proud of myself for actually completing a goal I had since high school. I was overjoyed about this accomplishment. Our marriage was suffering deeply, but I had told God I would withstand whatever came my way, infidelity included. I knew biblically, I didn't have to, but I have always been a forgiving person. I have always had this "savior complex" that has inflicted great wounds on me because I want to help everybody. I stood, well more like kneeled, because I was so tired. I was getting to the end of my rope and I was so sad that I would yet again be on the verge of disappointing God if I couldn't keep my word to Him.

I had entered a contest to be able to deliver the graduation speech for my graduating class and won. I can't even tell y'all how blessed I felt to be able to do this. The honor of being able to speak for my entire graduating class, in front of thousands of people, had given me an adrenaline rush. I was so excited to make the people I loved proud. To make my mom proud, my children, my Bishop, my pastor and most definitely, my husband. This was my person. However, that night, I had never been so disappointed in my life. I experienced a different type of heartbreak that night.

His car had been broken down. He stayed behind and didn't leave out with us to head to the convention center because he was waiting for someone to come to fix it. So, he told us to go ahead and he would be there as soon as it was done. I didn't want him to wait. I wanted him to go with me. I didn't want there to be a possibility of him missing the graduation. I needed him to support me. The kids and I go ahead without him, because I had to be there early. I couldn't afford to be late. We get downtown and I am walking into the convention center and my shoe breaks. I am a whole mess because I don't have any other shoes. Then, I remember that I had some sandals in my van. I go back and grab them and I have to wear them instead of the cute shoes I had picked out to match my cute outfit. I enter the facility and I take my place.

They have several seats on the front row blocked off for me, for my family members. My husband's seat was closest to the podium. I would be able to look out directly at him while I was addressing the audience. It would help calm my nerves because I was a nervous wreck. I had been so excited but now that the time had come, I wasn't sure I would be able to do this. Time kept inching closer to the start time. My mom was there, my sister and nephew, my cousins, several of my church family. The entire youth group had come from church to support me. It warmed my heart so much that people loved me enough to take time out of their schedule to be there for me. But there was a war within me that told me, he wasn't coming. He wasn't going to make it, and he didn't.

I gave my speech, I did my best, even with all of the emotions roaring inside of me. Even fighting back tears because I had to look at that empty seat the whole time while giving my speech. I had to look at that empty seat when I said "I want to thank my husband, my kids, my mom and all those who have supported me on this journey." I made that statement with bitterness growing in my throat as I spoke it. I was heartbroken at a different magnitude than I had ever been before. I couldn't believe he wouldn't show up. I couldn't believe I wasn't worth it. Such a monumental occasion in my life, yet I was unable to share it with "my person".

I smiled through all the congratulations and photo opportunities. I declined invitations to eat with people and do anything following the ceremony. My kids were working at Qdoba right near the convention center and so we decided to stop in there and grab food and then head home. As we began to walk there, I look up and there he is. He is holding some wilting flowers that he grabbed on his way there. He apologizes and tells me how he got turned around and couldn't find the place. I just look at him, smile, grab the flowers, walk past him and drop them in the trash. We went in Qdoba and ate. We got in the car and headed home when we were done. It was an eerily silent ride. I had decided I was done. I gave up on that car ride home. I couldn't withstand another thing. This, was my breaking point. I couldn't pretend to be happy anymore. I couldn't pretend that things were getting better, because they weren't. I no longer wanted to live like this and if alone was my consequence, so be it. I felt as if being alone had to be better than living in what seemed to be prison to me at the time. I figured it couldn't be any worse than the loneliness I felt right in that very moment.

In the following months, we hardly spoke. I had put in applications to move and we continued to argue. He continued to not come home for days at a time sometimes. I would stay in the bedroom most of the time and he would be in the living room. I finally got a letter stating that one of my applications for housing had been approved. I followed up with the people about it and planned to begin the process to leave. I never told him. I didn't want to argue anymore. I didn't want to fight anymore. It was my plan to just up and leave, hopefully one day while he was gone.

I remember our anniversary rolling around and he walked to my job, which wasn't far from our house, and delivered balloons and candy and stuff. My coworkers were so excited and happy about it. I, however, was nonchalant. They were so confused as to why I was not as excited as they were. They had no idea the turmoil I had been living in. I wasn't there when he delivered them. I had taken my lunch break and went to pick up food when he came. So, when I got home, he was livid. We had a huge argument about me not being there when he came and him making the effort to do such a nice gesture. It was too late for me. Niceties wasn't going to save all the damage that we had created over the last ten plus years. Those balloons and candy were not going to erase all the anniversaries, birthdays, and other special occasions before that, in which I had not received anything. I remember crying myself to sleep and asking God to just get me out of there. I was so unhappy I did not want to be there anymore because it was not only damaging him and I, it was damaging my kids as well. I wanted to do better for them.

A few weeks go by and I meet the lady to see the house she has for me. I pull up to this beautiful three-bedroom house, two and a half baths with an attached garage. I had never lived in a house like this before. I couldn't believe this was real. I couldn't believe that the same little girl from the projects was about to be able to rent a house like this. I signed the lease, got the keys and got a U-Haul. I was so anxious that he was going to come home and catch me moving out. I wasn't in the mood for another argument. I hadn't boxed anything because I didn't want him to know that we were leaving. He had been gone for a day or two so I thought I had time to get all my things and get out. I didn't. He showed up and saw that truck in the yard and was devastated. He was so angry with me. He was yelling and hurting from me not telling him I was leaving. He told me not to touch another thing. He packed the entire truck, by himself and he said "go, you want to leave me so bad, there, go and don't ever come back here again."

I got my kids. I put them all in the U-Haul and I left. I cried a thousand tears on that drive. I cried for the dissolution of my marriage. I cried for my kids and all they had endured and all they would have to endure with only having me. I cried for the years of heartache he and I caused one another. I cried for the unbearable brokenness that I felt. I cried from the depths of my soul at the thought of being alone forever. I had to. I had told God that if it didn't work, I would just have to suffer the consequences of being alone, so I had to. I couldn't go back on my word to God. That cry came from deep within me, because from a little girl, I never wanted to be alone. My kids set in silence as I drove. I'm sure they were sad too because I was but they were happy to be moving to a new house. They were happy to have a space where they didn't have to hear yelling at any given time during the day or night. They were happy that they would finally have the possibility of having a mother who was healthy enough to care about her appearance and heal from wounds that was causing them their own wounds. They were excited about a fresh start. Really, I was too. Even though I was in agonizing pain and my heart was disintegrating with every mile I drove, I too was excited to finally experience peace.

We pulled up at the new house and they were so excited about it. They couldn't believe this was our home. When I unlocked the door and pushed it open, peace flooded me. There was peace in this house. There was a fresh start and a new beginning awaiting us. We got some comforters off of the truck and a couple pillows and we lay there on the living room floor together thanking God for this blessing and we slept, good.

The next day my church members came and helped us unload the truck. We got settled in and some of the heaviness of my decision was beginning to lift a bit. I lived there for a while before I ever even let him know where we lived. I still checked on him. I still made sure he was ok, for years to come. I felt obligated to because he had already lost so much in his life.

I left, but I stayed connected to him. This is how the enemy will trap us. When we decide to turn away from something, we must turn away completely. We can't continue to dabble with what we are delivered from because it will only cause us more trauma. If God says to "kill everything", we can't keep trying to keep dead things on life support with our actions. The consequences of that will be that it will come back to bite us (1 Samuel 15:1-35). If God is calling for a disconnect, you must completely disconnect from what He is calling you away from. Otherwise, you will have to suffer the consequence of rebelling against what He has commanded you to do.

I hadn't completely moved on from our marriage, because our divorce still hadn't been filed yet. I began to think, ok maybe God can still change him. We were just separated and, in my heart, I was hoping that would wake him up. I was hoping that he would see I wasn't playing and decide, ok, I want to live for God. If I don't, then I lose her. I don't have the authority to place an ultimatum like that on anyone. I cannot negotiate anyone's salvation for them. That is something they have to want and they have to take to God themselves. Oh, how foolish I was to think that I could "trick" someone into living for God and loving me the way I felt I deserved to be loved. Nobody could fix that but Jesus. However, Jesus would only fix it when they were ready and not a moment sooner.

He didn't change, because we can't choose for people. Everyone has to answer their own call, we can't answer it for them. I remember having a conversation with my pastor and he said to me, "Gina, as long as he has Gina, he will never seek Jesus. Why would he if you continue to be his savior?"

That hit me like a ton of bricks. It was painful to watch him hurt; this was the person I was supposed to love and adore for the rest of my life. I didn't want to see him in pain. However, after that talk, I began to let go. I had to. I could no longer try to stand in the place of Jesus. Who am I? I went and got a divorce packet and completed it all and filed my motion in the courts myself. When he got the letter in the mail, he called me angry and upset that I would have the audacity to file for a divorce. We had been separated for almost two years at this time. I don't know why he was so surprised. He had a girlfriend and everything, but he refused to sign the papers. I filed for a default judgment because in our state, I didn't need his signature. The divorce was eventually granted and I was free. So, why didn't I feel free? Why did I feel as if I was experiencing a living death? Why was my heart, daily, threatening to burst out of my chest? Why was I crying myself to sleep every night, if I was free?

This didn't feel like freedom. It felt like another form of bondage. I was suffocating. I was tired of fighting. I decided I wasn't going to fight anymore. The enemy had done a number on me with this one. I knew it was coming, so I'm not sure why I reacted in this way but I wasn't prepared for the emotional scars that would come with this. I went to a really dark place. A place of prayerlessness. A place of unforgiveness. A place of bitterness. A place of offense. A place of brokenness like I had never experienced before. I lost my will to pray, to speak those things as though they were (Romans 4:16-22 KJV) and I had begun to stagger at the promises of God.

That's the worst thing we can do when we are in a dark place or a rough storm. We cannot be afraid to speak out and ask for help. Number one, in prayer. Number two, get you some genuine people in your corner who aren't afraid to go to war for you and will always speak life into you when all you can feel is death! It's a dangerous place to be, in the dark alone. Don't let the enemy abuse your mind. Evict him by the power that is in the blood and the name of Jesus Christ! I'm so very thankful for my covering. They are the real deal. My pastor and Bishop do not play about me and I don't play about them. When I was spiritually anemic, unable to fight for myself, they were iron for me. You know what the Bible says about iron, right (Proverbs 27:17)?

"That's where I was wrong. That is the wrong mindset to have in the kingdom of God. We don't do this because we have to, we do this because we get to."

I began to walk in a season of dark wilderness. I didn't even know who I was. I never missed a service. I was at church faithfully, in the flesh. However, my spirit was a million miles away. Some days, my eldest daughter would threaten to call my pastor in order to get me out of the bed. I just didn't want to live that life anymore if I wasn't going to see any returns on my investments. If I wasn't going to get anything back off of what I was giving, what was I doing?

That's where I was wrong. That is the wrong mindset to have about the kingdom of God. We don't do this because we have to, we do this because we get to. We get to serve God, we get to love God, we get to bless others and have others bless us. We do not do this as a "this for that" transaction type of relationship. God wants all of us. He can't use us without us relinquishing all of ourselves to Him. We should not enter our relationship with God, with a "what's in it for me" mentality, but yet a "what can I allow God to do in and through me" type of mentality.

I went through a season of questioning all that I had learned. I went through a season of defeat and despair that I never want to experience ever again. I got to a point where I couldn't stop myself. It didn't matter that I knew I was living in sin. I would pray sometimes before and after committing sinful acts. I would repent and ask for forgiveness and still go right back to that same pool of vomit I kept asking God to save me from. I had no will to fight because I just couldn't believe that I had gotten a divorce. I had failed, tremendously, at something God honored so much.

I had changed my look. I kept my hair and nails done. I got a new wardrobe; a new home and a new vehicle. I was living the life now. I was no longer invisible. People were constantly telling me how beautiful I was, how talented I was and how wanted I was. People wanted me in their circles and men wanted to "take care of me". I had been missing this all of my life. This recognition was new. My flesh was soaking it up. I was too blind to see the tactics of the enemy at work in all of this. All I knew was I was no longer an outcast, no longer the last one picked, no longer the one that nobody wanted. It saddens me recalling this season of my life. I wasted so much time living in my flesh that God could have used to elevate me spiritually to use me for His kingdom.

We don't even realize that the enemy has devices that will cause us to believe that we are blessed all while living in a curse. This is where I was in this season. I was living in such rebellion to what I had come to know. The thing I had begun to hold so near and dear to my heart, I just laid it down. The worse part of it all is that I was only fooling myself that entire time. During the day, I would be living a lie; but at night, the truth would wreck me and come out in waves of emotion and soak every pillow on my bed. Insanity clearly sat in because I would live in a vicious cycle of this same merry-go-round for a while.

I got to a point where I didn't have a spiritual pulse anymore. I would go to church and sit in the back of the sanctuary close to the door and wear such a disgusting scowl on my face so no one would even want to talk to me. I didn't want to hear them trying to convict me of living the way I had been living. As soon as service was over, I was out the door. None of this was me. I am an extrovert. I usually sat in the middle rows or closer and I always chatted with somebody after service. Not in this season. In this season, I didn't like anyone. None of them could see the pain I was in and they didn't care about it either. Why would I try to hold a conversation with people who didn't care about me?

Let me interject something right here. The most valuable lesson I learned in this season is that I couldn't keep waiting until my house was on fire to try to put fires out. I needed to be taking the necessary precautions to keep my house from becoming hazardous in the first place. I was allowing things to develop into emergent situations instead of handling them when they were urgent. I was employing God as my own personal 911 operator, the nerve. When things got bad, I wanted to run and call Him to send first responders to rescue me when I should have been taking preventative measures to keep from allowing my life to get so far off track. Preventative measures of consistency, faithfulness, prayer, studying, fasting and connecting with Him. Instead, I held Him at a distance in the form of a red reset button on my desk to dig me out of pits I was digging for myself. God is not a genie in a bottle. He is much more than that, much more powerful than that and we need to always treat our relationship with Him as such. I promise you that you would have much more quality of life living with Him at the head.

Running your decisions by Him first would always benefit us more than if we address Him after the fact. If I had of made the decision to keep going to God about my heartbreak, my disappointments, and my grief over the troubles in my life instead of turning to men who had no power to change me, I would have realized that He could and He would have rescued me much sooner. Looking back now, I understand that going through that season birthed a victor in me I never knew lived inside of me. So, I'm thankful for it. However, if I could have done it differently, I most definitely would have.

I kept doing this for about a year and a half. Routinely attending church, not retaining anything. Not praying at home. Allowing my Bible to collect dust as if it was on a hidden shelf in an antique shop. I kept going places I knew I shouldn't go. Talking to people I knew I shouldn't talk to. My flesh was craving love. The love I never experienced from my biological father. The love I was missing out on now since I was divorced. The love I had unfortunately come to the realization of that I had never even experienced before. So, I settled for the substitute of lust. It was the next best thing.

Typing this now, I see that I was so lost. It hurts my heart that I stayed in that place for so long. How blessed am I that God saw fit to allow me to make it out? I could have died in that pit. My God! However, I didn't. I am alive today because my Father had a coat waiting for me.

I remember one day just being tired. I was just exhausted from living in two worlds. I was weary from allowing myself to join the victim team again after tasting so many victories. I had stopped going to services at the main campus because I just was no longer interested in hearing about all the good things of God that never seemed to happen for me. I didn't want to hear about how God was moving for everybody else when He wasn't moving for me. I didn't want to hear about His goodness, when it didn't seem as if He was being good to me. How foolish I was. This is a fine example of why we must always guard our hearts and minds because once we allow the enemy to plant a seed of deception within us, it is the hardest fight of our lives to get that seed uprooted.

Again, I had stopped going to services at main campus, but that day, weariness pushed me to go. I recall walking in and sitting on the far side of the building closest to the drum cage. As I sat on the pew and my eyes surfed around the sanctuary I was bewildered as to why I was there. I sat there in a room full of people but I was deathly alone. I contemplated leaving this place, this sanctuary, that had saved me a many of times before. I looked up to the pulpit and watched as the praise team sang and I became angry that they didn't understand where I was. They didn't care, no one did. They weren't experiencing the problems that I was experiencing and so they couldn't possibly imagine my storm. I thought, what's the use? I'm messed up right now anyway. I turned my eyes to my Bishop, now standing in the pulpit and looked back at my First Lady seated behind me a section over a few rows back. They didn't understand I said. Then, he called me. "Sis Gina, I need you to come and stand right here," as he pointed to the altar area directly below him right in front of the pulpit. I didn't think twice. I didn't hesitate to move because if I had of, I wouldn't have been able to take a step in that direction at all. I stood immediately and placed my hands in the pockets of my jean jacket as I walked to that place. My spirit was leading me because my flesh was deceiving me and telling me I would literally fall in front of everyone. I wouldn't make it. I wasn't sure how I would make it those 50 steps to the front but my soul was in jeopardy, so I pushed.

"The well that had been dug in my spirit, all those years ago begin to have some movement. There was activity there. There was living water churning inside of me."

Someone else may have felt as if they were being put under a magnifying glass for others to see their flaws, their struggles and their disappointments, but I didn't care. While others may have been angered, frustrated, embarrassed, even offended by what was taking place, I was not. I was not because I was actually thankful to be standing in front of the very people, I had come to call family. That quick, they turned from enemy to ally. I quickly remembered who they were and that they did care for me. My fragility in that moment, pushed me. The seeds that had been previously planted on the inside were reminding me of where I could find peace. The well that had been dug in my spirit, years ago begin to have some movement. There was activity there. There was living water churning inside of me. I felt as if my spirit stood naked in front of a whole congregation of people and I could care less, because my soul was hurting. My soul was in danger, so, I was willing to try whatever it took to shake myself! That hadn't been the plan when I walked in. I wasn't even sure why I had gone, because I didn't even want to be there. I had unconsciously drove there and walked into that sanctuary, hoping that someone there would get a heavy burden on them and stand in the gap for me in a season where I was unable to stand for myself. I was welcoming that because of the place that I was in, I was wanting somebody to help dig me out because I didn't have the tools to do it alone! God provided a means of escape for me yet again. He drove me there. He walked me to that altar and He met me there. I am forever indebted to Him for His grace. It has been absolutely sufficient over my life.

I stood there, looking down as he spoke to me. Finally, I mustered up the courage to look up and listen as he spoke. There was always authority in his voice. God has given him such a special anointing and I'm blessed to be covered by someone who refuses to just sit and watch people go to hell, but instead will clear your path to give you the chance to choose the will of God. There is a healthy fear of God that seems to consume you whenever you're around him. Well for me anyway. I have no earthly idea how anyone could be in his presence and lie to his face or not take heed to his words. It's as if you come into contact with the heart of God when he speaks, whether it is teaching, preaching, correcting or prophesying in faith over your life. There is a peace that I always automatically feel when listening to him. This time was no different. He spoke life into me at that moment. I knew it was God because no one knew the fight that I was in. No one knew how much it took just to get me there. But, God did and He met me there. Tears streamed, rushing down my cheeks because again, he came for me.

You see because we had been here before. I had gotten offended about some things that had happened and stopped going to church for a while. I was not about to attend a church that had let me down. Just like our flesh, huh? Fleshly thinking will always have us committing spiritual suicide. We have to be mindful of our thoughts and our tongues, especially when it's what we are thinking or speaking towards ourselves. It is not "the church" that lets us down, it's people. It's humans. It's out of control flesh that is unsubmitted to the things of God. They always will, and so will we. We will let other people down ourselves also. We have to choose to forgive, every time. Then we have to pray that we are also forgiven when the tables turn and we are the ones needing forgiveness. The church is not spotless, because flesh is there; however, it should be healthy enough to address wounds and nurse them back to health and not let others bleed to death right in front of you. I didn't even give the situation a chance. In my flesh, I just stopped going.

So, one day, I had planned a rest day. I hadn't planned to leave the house, but my mom called and she needed me to do something for her so I got ready to go to her house. I walked down my stairs and opened my door and there stood Pastor Nichols (now the Bishop). I was shocked and surprised to see him. He said he had been ringing the doorbell but I had not heard anything and that doorbell was always extremely loud. The enemy is a sly ole fox and he was trying his best to keep me from having this encounter. However, God is always orchestrating things just as He wants them done. He had my mother call me right in that exact moment because He knew I needed to open the door. God refused to allow me to miss an encounter that would get me back on the right path.

"Hey, Pastor, what you doing here?" I asked with a nervous undertone.
"Hey, it's been a while. I don't even fully know all the details, or what brought about your absence, but what I do know is that you know that this is not how we fight. I will see you at service on Sunday."

He turned and began walking back to his vehicle.

"Yes sir," I mumbled loud enough for him to hear. I turned and locked my door and waited until he was gone to walk towards my vehicle to get in to leave. I had never had anyone notice my absence. I most definitely had not ever had anyone notice my absence and then come to find out why I was absent in person. I had never had anyone care so much for my soul that they would beckon me to try God again. This man of God was the real deal. He proved to me that he would always come for me and any other sheep in his fold that decided to be "THE ONE". At this moment, he knew that the 99 were not the issue at that time. I was ready to give up. I was ready to quit. But, God said no!

That night, standing in that altar below the pulpit listening to him plead the blood over my life and speak to the well within me, caused those memories to flood back to my mind so quickly. I couldn't just lay here in this valley. I wasn't created to quit. I wasn't built to give up. So, I decided right then and there that I wouldn't give up, instead, I would GET UP!!!

That night, I went home and decided I wasn't living like this anymore. I was retrieving my birthright, my kid's birthright, my mama's birthright and anybody else's that God wanted me to snatch out of the enemy's hands. If it wasn't of

God, it wasn't getting my attention. I started praying again. I remember overhearing my kids on the phone saying "oh that's my mom, she's praying". It tickled me to hear them explain to their friends what all that ruckus was about in the background. I had rekindled a fire of an altar that I had once allowed to burn out. I vowed, never again. However, in experiencing recent trials, I understand that my vows and prayers must always be sifted through God's hands first. Meaning, I have to consult God before I make any plans or vows to anything. I have to say "God, what do You want from me? Teach me, mold me, help me be all that You want me to be always. I pray, that You would always keep Your hands on my life, my mind, my heart and spirit so it remains right, even in tribulation." I say this because trouble will come, though it won't last, it will come. Sometimes, in trouble, we forget the vows and promises that we have made to God. We focus on the pain, the problem, the issue, instead of the one who can relieve us of it. This is where we go wrong. We have to keep our eyes on the promise keeper because He is also the problem solver. Our problems are not too big for Him.

I recently had a conversation where I was asked to share something with a group. I decided to talk about beauty for ashes. I told them how I had for far too long focused on the lump of ashes beneath me, instead of the hill above me where my help comes from. I cannot sit in the wreckage of my choices, the enemy's devices or any other thing set in my path to destroy me. I must instead focus on the beauty that is to come from those ashes. Ashes are not just ashes. Inside the pile of destruction that we see, God is working something for our good. He is molding what we see as destitute, meaningless and damaged, into something anointed, beautiful and powerful. I am so thankful for the ashes that He made beauty out of in my life.

Slowly, I regained my footing. I began to mend relationships I had broken in my season of isolation. I'm not sure that I had broken them really, but had put them on autopilot and hadn't allowed them into my life in the same capacity that they once were. However, I came to the realization that I needed the strength of others who were stronger than me in this season to help me fight. I was spiritually anemic, and I needed iron. I joined up in the spirit with a couple at church and we started doing these power hour Bible studies anytime we could. Their house, my house, restaurants, wherever we could get in the word, we did. It was putting so much strength back into my body. I can't even explain what those sessions were doing for me. Breaking bread, getting in the word of God, with other people and getting excited about the things of God again is a feeling I can't even put into words for you.

I can tell you that worthlessness began to fall off of me daily. Condemnation, shame, guilt and heaviness all took their exit one by one. God did a new thing in my life and I am today, forever grateful that He just keeps choosing me. Even when I feel like the last to be picked, the unworthy one, the person with the least pedigree, He chooses me. He continues to remind me every day that I am His. He cannot fail, so therefore there can be no failure in me because He lives in me. I refuse to claim a title He eradicated at Calvary. He gave His life so that I could live. I refuse to live without Him. I refuse to live without telling the world about Him. I once was lost, but now I'm found.

I spent a season in the pigpen. It was of my own recognizance. I was never meant to abide with swine, unfortunately, I let my guard down and I found myself there. However, the moment I decided that was not where I belonged, He welcomed me home. He stood afar off and rejoiced at the sight of my return. He gave me beauty for ashes. He gave me another chance to be free in Him. How can I live this life as if I'm estranged from my Father when He is omnipresent in my life? Everywhere I go, He is there. Everything I see, I see Him in it. I am not an orphan. I am no longer a fatherless child because my Father has welcomed me back into the fold again. He has given me a torch to carry for those around me to see that they are welcome here also. He has tasked me with the great honor of sharing His gospel to the world. He has given me a testimony filled with transparency in hopes that someone else doesn't fall into the same pits I did.

Now, every day, I start my day thankful for His grace and mercy. I start my day anew and try to make Him proud in all my deeds. I can't live in yesterday's mistakes; I have to live for tomorrow's adventures. He has promised me life more abundantly and every day I up my expectancy level to receive all that He has for me. In doing that, I have to be willing to accept and give an honest no to those things that I know don't belong in my life. I have come to the realization that an honest no makes way for a sincere yes. The only way you can give your best yes is if you can give an honest no. This is the same with God. Sometimes God will give us a no, that is making room for His yes. It could be the right place, but the wrong time, right person, wrong time, right situation but the wrong time. Timing is everything with God. I trust His timing. Amazing grace, how sweet the sound. I once was lost, but now I'm found. I am God's prized possession. I am His selfie, beautifully and wonderfully made in His image. There is nothing this world can offer me now to keep me from believing that. He has proven to me now, time and time again, who I am and who He is in my life. I don't have any other choice but to believe it. I've seen too much. I've experienced too much not to. This chapter is only a snippet of my story. It is only a commercial of the full motion picture of all that He has done for me. I hope I have done the name of the Lord justice enough to snatch another one from the pit of hell. I hope it is enough to prick the heart of someone in a valley so dark and deep somewhere to call them out of it. I hope it is enough to beckon another vagabond, to come home.

Let me say this. If you have wandered away from God, please do all that you can to find your way back to Him. He is waiting with open arms to welcome you home. He is waiting for you to come to the realization of the error of your ways and to return unto Him. He is waiting to have compassion on you and hug your neck and kiss your forehead to let you know that His love still remains. He is waiting to call for a celebration of your return. He has a robe awaiting you, a fatted calf and shoes for your feet. There is always a place for you at His feet, in His pasture and in His kingdom. All you have to do is choose to return to Him. I know this because more than once, I left my Father's house. I chose to abide in a foreign land that I was never meant to travel to. I chose to become roadkill because I had decided to travel a road that was never meant to be my path. Along the way, in my weary state, while I was slowly drifting, I met a man. He beckoned for me to come. He called for me to come and I did. It is the best decision I could have ever made. I'm just so honored that He would see me as worthy of His blood. That He would see fit to deem me worthy of His love. There is no greater love than this, that a man would lay his life down for his friend (John 15:13 KJV). I could never thank Him enough for all that He has done for me. However, I know for a fact, that He wants to and He can and He will do it for you too.

Understand this. Though I lay with pigs for that season; though I spent all that I had, wasted all that I had in that season; in this season, I am prospering. In this season, I am recovering all that I lost, plus interest. In this season, I am finally

home, where I belong. In my Father's house.
There is room for you too. You can come home. I
am a ProdiGAL! **And I, am here to stay!**

EPILOGUE

Wow! What a powerful read? Thank each and every one of you for going on this journey with these Daughters of Destiny. It is the prayer of every author involved in this book that someone's heart is pricked and begins longing for a touch from Jesus. It was the goal and vision of each of these ladies to share some of the darkest moments of their lives, not to give any credit to the enemy who seeks to kill, steal and destroy (John 10:10 KJV), but to glorify the power of the almighty God, Jesus Christ.

The stories in this book are to bring glory and honor to God. Showcasing His omnipotence and His exuberant power. He always works all things together for the good of those that love Him (Romans 8:28 KJV). The testimonies in this book are evidence of who God is to each of us. Life will happen to us; however, we have to be strong enough and bold enough to continue to stand on the promises and word of God to make it through each of our trials.

Condemnation and shame are of the devil. It is not of God. It is when we allow ourselves to be bound by these things that we are unable to fight in the posture needed to win certain battles in our lives. God is always a present help in our time of trouble. We have to know when to call on Him. We also have to know how to fight these battles. We are equipped with everything we need to overcome any obstacle set in our paths by the enemy. Revelations 12:11 AMP says, "And they overcame and conquered him because of the blood of the Lamb and because of the word of their testimony, for they did not love their life and renounce their faith even when faced with death."

Some of the stories you heard in this book definitely had these women facing death, but they didn't relent. They squared their shoulders, planted their feet and stood! With the right posture, and with Christ (Philippians 4:13 KJV), we can do anything! Ephesians 6:11 AMP Put on the full armor of God (for His precepts are like the splendid armor of a heavily-armed soldier), so that you may be able to (successfully) stand up against all the schemes and the strategies and the deceits of the devil.

These women showed you, me, us, the readers, that God is always by our sides. God is always protecting us, even from ourselves sometimes. There is no God like Jesus. He is Alpha and Omega, beginning and the end, the first and the last (Revelations 22:13 KJV). He cares for us. Even when we don't seem to care for ourselves, He shows His grace, love and mercy. These things allow us to come back from the brinks of death more times than some of us even deserve.

If the testimonies on these pages don't do something to your heart, what will? So often we go through trials and we believe, it's just us alone. These stories prove that you are not alone. There are other people out here who have experienced the same things you have and others who have experienced worse but have been renewed in mind and spirit because they decided to answer His call. They decided to choose Jesus. With that, they have been rejuvenated, restored and redeemed to even better than they were before they encountered the worse trials and tribulations of their lives. Who wouldn't want to live a life unto God?

These chapters are simply that, chapters of the lives of a group of beautifully brilliant women who love God first. These women have allowed God to author their lives and continue to live out His will as the lead character of the stories of their lives. These women, who the enemy was determined to make victims out of, have become the victors God had always destined them to be.

Hopefully the words leapt off the pages of this book and into the deep crevices of your heart causing a tsunamic eruption that propels you into a walk with God like you've never had before. May you begin a new walk, placing one foot in front of the other, on a new journey to destiny with the King. Prayerfully, these words will encourage you to now tell your story to someone else in hopes of releasing them from their own prisons of insanity. This is how we live when we are in the world; in a constant state of insanity. We continue to try the same things, (fornication, drugs, alcohol, rebellion and other gruesome sinful ways), yet expect a different outcome in our lives. This is foolishness. In order to experience change, you have to make a change.

Make a decision today to walk away from the world. Make a decision today to walk into the kingdom of God. He is waiting for you to return home. It is your destiny to dwell with your father, the King. You can be a ProdiGAL too; all you have to do is choose to come on home!

Thank You

Special thanks to the friends and family members of each author in this book who has prayed, supported and encouraged each of us to live this life for Christ. To those of you who know some of the deepest, darkest times and secrets of our lives, thank you. We are all thankful for the prayers of the righteous because without you all, there would be no us. To our parents who brought us in this world and taught us lessons of what to do and what not to do and did their very best to raise us the best they could, thank you. To grandparents, who loved us when it seemed as if no one else in the world did, thank you. To our leadership that is always standing in the gap for us and encouraging us to be our best selves in Christ, thank you. To our supporters, which includes everyone that will purchase, read, and gift this book to someone else, thank you. To our children, for making us better women of God by challenging us each and every day to stay the course, if for no other reason but to make sure that they have an example of what a godly life looks like, thank you. To everyone. Thank you. It is our hearts desire and our deepest prayer that this book not just be words on these pages, but that this book would be a lifeline that someone else may see the goodness of God and want to try Him for themselves. Words are not enough to do justice to the gratitude we hold for your support and for God's grace. May the blessings of the Lord be upon you forevermore.

Be on the lookout, because the ProdiGAL story is not over. In fact, it has just begun.

Made in the USA
Middletown, DE
09 October 2022

12323315R00176